THE LAST OF THE ONION MEN

The Last of the Onion Men

Gwyn Griffiths

ISBN: 0-86381-783-1

Cover design: Sian Parri

First published in Welsh in 2002 by
Gwasg Carreg Gwalch, 12 Iard yr Orsaf, Llanrwst, Wales LL26 0EH
℡ 01492 642031   📠 01492 641502
🖰 books@carreg-gwalch.co.uk   Internet: www.carreg-gwalch.co.uk

French language translation by Josseline Mondot.

Published by Les Editions Le Télégramme,
19 rue Jean Macé, BP 118, 29867 Brest, Breizh.

Printed in Wales.

Contents

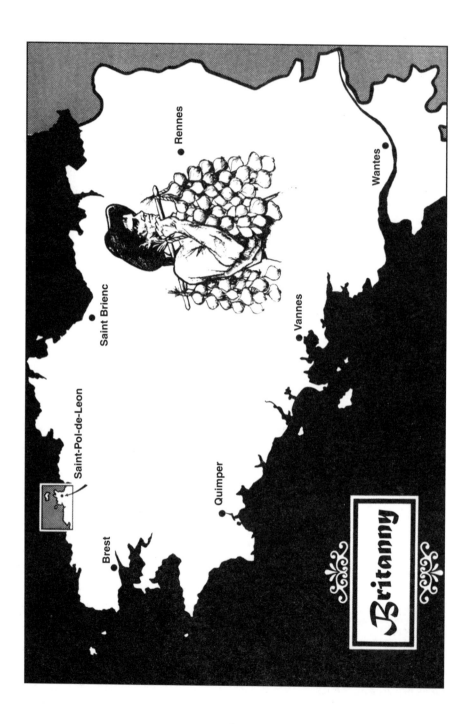

Rennes

Wantes

Saint Brienc

Vannes

Saint-Pol-de-Leon

Quimper

Brest

Britanny

6

Introduction

W. Ambrose Bebb, a Welsh writer who wrote extensively about Brittany between the two Wars, described the first time he saw the Johnny Onion Men in his book *Pererindodau* ('Pilgrimages'). He was, he said, five years of age and travelling with his parents in a horse and cart to the annual autumn fair at the village of Pontrhydfendigaid in Ceredigion. "... powerful, broad-shouldered men in blue trowsers and wooden shoes – clogs," he said. "Each one with a thick stick cut from a hedge on his shoulder from which hung rows of gleaming Breton onions."

If Bebb was correct that he was five years of age at the time, the year would have been 1899. He continued, affectionately. "Johnny Onions – the only visitor who comes to Wales respectfully, humbly, gentlemanly ... the only true aristocrats to visit us during a year."

In another chapter he describes walking in the direction of Roscoff and a man with a horse and cart invites him to ride with him to the town. The man in the cart turns out to be a Johnny Onion Man who used to come to Llanelli in Wales. From then on they conversed in Welsh. The Johnny talking about the miseries of tramping through wind and rain, in wet clothes from morning to night, about people in Wales who thought they were tramps.

In spite of such occasional impressions, the onion men were known and welcomed in every corner of England, Scotland and Wales. I would like to think that they received the warmest, fondest welcome in Wales. There was not in Wales a town or village that was not at one time regularly visited by a Johnny. Even based in the town. I regularly learn of some new centre where the Johnnies had a base, stringing and selling their onions. I have never seen Pontypridd mentioned on any list as a place where the Johnnies had a centre. Yet older people who have lived in the town all their lives tell me they remember the Johnnies based in the stables at the back of the White Hart, a hotel in the centre of the town. Others remember them working under the railway arches by the town's station. They might have lived and slept there too. A middle-aged woman who had a vegetable stall in Pontypridd Market told me she used to rent one of her storehouses to the Johnnies.

At one time there were many Johnnies based in Cardiff, but one had been based at Tongwynlais, the first village outside Cardiff on the road to Merthyr. There were others based in the Rhondda Valley.

It has been claimed that a high percentage of the Johnnies – in proportion to size and population – came to Wales. The point being that Welsh and Breton are sister langages. It is certainly true that generations of Welsh poets have praised the onion men.

"... ef yw'r unig fargeiniwr ar daith

A edrydd degwch ei lwyth yn eich iaith, -

A chofiwch – perthynas i chwi yw'r gŵr,

Mae'r gwaed o hyd yn dewach ma'r dŵr."

" ... he is the only
                    salesman abroad
Who in your language
                    praises his load, -
And always remember
– this man is your brother,
Blood is always
                    thicker than water."

So wrote T. Eirug Davies.

Eifion Wyn wrote "Yr Alltud" (The Exile) an elegy to a 15-year-old Breton buried in a grave on the edge of Porthmadog, never visited and no flowers placed on it apart from those shed by the black thorn in the spring. I have been told that the boy was a Johnny.

The farmer-poet Isfoel expressed relief when Johnny returned safely after the dark days of World War II.

Dylan Thomas weaved a delightfully accurate cameo of a Johnny in one of his short stories:

"A Shoni-onion Breton man, with a beret and a necklace of onions, bicycled down the road and stopped at the door.
"'Quelle un grand matin, monsieur,' I said.
"'There's French for you, boy bach!' he said."

Many retired Johnnies told me of the welcome they received in Scotland and England. But I have been unable to find poets, other than from Wales, who sang their praises.

The onions of the Johnnies de Roscoff were more highly prized in Britain than in Paris. Even in their own district of Roscoff the Johnnies themselves did not always receive the respect they deserved. One old Johnny told me how they were considered to be at the lower end of Roscoff's social scale. But as their trade comes to an end they are finally getting the acknowledgement for their contribution to the economy of what was once an impoverished area.

Since the end of the 1970s and the beginning of the 1980s books began to appear piecing together a picture of their lives and history. In 1995 a small museum opened in Roscoff, a tribute to their colourful – and sometimes sad – history. Ironically, the idea was conceived and the panels presenting their story were done in Wales. But this was not, perhaps, that strange bearing in mind the respect and affection with which they were held in Wales, England and Scotland.

Gwyn Griffiths

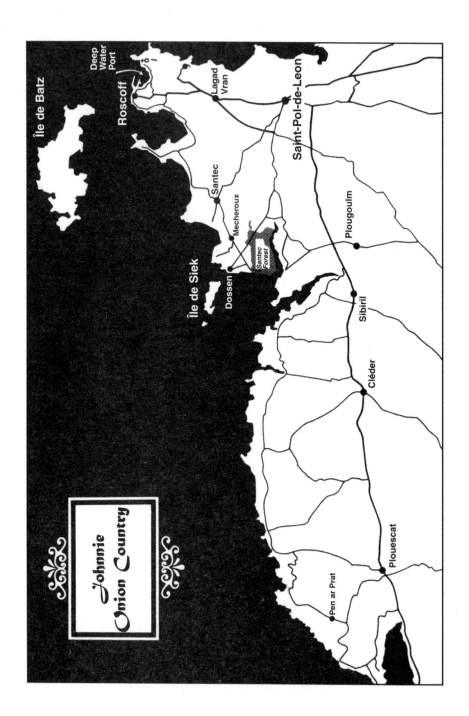

île de Batz

Deep Water Port

Roscoff

Lagad Vran

Saint-Pol-de-Leon

Santec

Mecheroux

Santec Forest

Plougoulm

île de Siek

Dossen

Sibiril

Cléder

Johnnie Onion Country

Pen ar Prat

Plouescat

Chapter 1

Johnny Onions

For 170 years men with exotic accents selling beautifully platted strings of onions have knocked doors in England, Scotland and Wales. At one time they were a familiar sight from John O'Groats to Lands End, from the Shetlands to the Channel Islands. Before World War II there was a company of onion sellers based on Stornoway and there were companies on The Isle of Man and The Isle of Wight. Johnny Onions was, most of the time, a well-loved character, a popular figure in town and country.

Johnny Onions to the English, *Ingan Johnnie* to the Scots, *Shoni Onions* or *Shoni Winwns* to the Welsh. They took back with them to Roscoff, in north-western Brittany, the name by which they were known in Britain. They are the *Johnnies de Roscoff*, or – in this predominantly Breton-speaking area – Ar *Johniged*. The reason for the nickname is that many were called Jean, or Jean-Yves. Yves, favourite saint of the Bretons, is a popular name in Brittany.

The arrival of Johnny Onions around the end of August was a sign that the winter months were drawing closer. He was no less popular for that, or at least not when I first remember them. But at one time there had been, one old seller told me, far too many of them coming over. By the end of the 1920s and the beginning of the 1930s, 1,500 of them made the annual migration for six months hard work in the most miserable of living conditions.

Today the numbers have dwindled to about a dozen. Most of them work on their own – Jean Le Roux goes to Highbury in London, Guillaume Seité now in his 80s comes to Bristol for a few months, François Keriven does a full season in Leeds, Paul Caroff and his wife come over to Poole for the odd fortnight or a month in the autumn. Another goes to Southampton and sells for a full season.

The only "company" left comes to Cardiff. Patrick Mevel took up the trade with his grandfather in the early 1980s at a time when most of the old Johnnies were giving up. He employs five or six young men, often students taking a year out to improve their English. From their base in an old shop in Grangetown, Cardiff, Patrick and his company visit most of Wales and parts of the west of England.

The First Johnny

The most celebrated, and the first, Johnny was Henri Olivier a peasant-sailor from the coastal village of Santec, west of Roscoff. He was born in 1808, his father died when he was 16 and his mother died three years later. He, his two brothers and a sister, were left in charge of the small farm. He was adventurous, but poverty was a greater incentive than any desire for adventure.

Before he was 20 he had travelled the length and breadth of Brittany with his horse and cart selling the vegetables he grew on his farm. He made a trip to Paris and established contact with restauranteurs, something which was to continue for decades.

But it was in 1828 that he made the most adventurous move of all. With four friends he hired a boat, loaded it with the local onions and sailed from Roscoff to Plymouth. Within a week they were back, they had sold the onions and their pockets were stuffed with sovereigns. Henri Olivier and his friends had hit on a new market giving new hope to an impoverished area and re-new trade links that were to last for well over a century. And, perhaps, inspire further contact closer to our own times in the form of Brittany Ferries.

There was a tradition of selling strings of onions in the Roscoff area going back at least to the 16th century. The onion sellers who followed Henri Olivier revived the tradition. By 1860, 200 Johnnies were making the annual journey to Britain, 700 in 1887, 1273 in 1902, 1152 in 1905, 1200 in 1907, 1300 in 1909, 1500 in 1931.

Henri Olivier made just one journey in 1828. He married a rich widow and it appears that he had no need to engage in such enterprises again. They had three children and he died in 1865. A street has been named after his family in Santec.

Johnny Country

The furthest point of Johnny Onions' country can be reached in 30 minutes by car from Roscoff. The land around Roscoff, Saint-Pol-de-Leon, and west as far as Plouescat is fertile and sandy. A string of islets and small islands give shelter from the northerly winds and the Gulf Stream ensures a warm climate. Frost is rare and the temperature rarely drops below six degrees Celsius. The rain is usually a fine persistent drizzle soaking the soil.

For centuries, travel writers have commented on the fertility of the area. Jacques Cambry, from Lorient in southern Brittany, wrote in his *Voyage dans le Finistère* in 1794: "The inhabitants of Roscoff cultivate the most fertile and fruitful land. It produces an incredible quantity of all kinds of vegetables; onions, cauliflowers, cabbages, artichokes, turnips, enough to provide for the whole of Finistère."

Gustave Flaubert, on a journey in Brittany in 1847, described it as "... the most fertile corner of Brittany. The Roscovite is a fortunate farmer, his field is his fortune ..."

"You can be harvesting carrots eight months of the year," the late Michel Olivier of Mecheroux once told me. "You can survive on ten acres of land here, in the rest of Brittany you need 45 acres to make a living."

Gilbert Guillou, Chairman of the Onion Growers Group of the SICA (*Société d'Initiative de Coopéeration Agricole*), once told me: "This area is the best in France – perhaps in Europe – for a young man with little capital to start farming. It's probably the only place possible to able to start from scratch."

Nowhere in the whole of Brittany is the hand of the farmer more evident. Hedges have been cleared and every square foot of land, often to the edge of the roads, is cultivated. The fertilizer is the seaweed raked up from the beaches, spread over the ground and ploughed in. The iodine from the seaweed gives the onions sold by the Johnnies their unique colour – a light rose colour.

An old onion seller, Jean-Marie Roignant, who worked in Caernarfon, Jersey and Perth, told me that seeds from anywhere in the world could be sown in the Johnnies countryside and when harvested the onion would always be the same reddish colour.

Roscoff – Capital of the Johnnies

Roscoff today is a busy, thriving little town. Solid buildings bear witness to a wealthy past – a past built on trade. Sea salt from Le Croisic in southern Brittany, salted fish, flax, sail cloth, cotton, wool, timber all came and went through the port of Roscoff. In the middle ages the town was trading with England, Portugal, Spain, Scandinavia, Latvia, Estonia. Old records reveal that vegetables were also exported to English ports from Roscoff during the 14th century. And the people of the town were selling their garden produce to foreign sailors in the port. The Capuchin Order settled in Roscoff in

1622 and it is believed that they were the first to introduce onions to the area.

It was a cosmopolitan town and agents from many countries settled there. There had been troubles – the English attacked and destroyed the town in 1347 and 1387. The Bretons retaliated in 1403 and 1404 by sacking Plymouth and Dartmouth. But despite the odd skirmish Roscoff preferred to be on good trading terms with the English. Brittany lost its political independence in 1532 but this had little or no effect on trade and the Breton corsairs, notably of Saint-Malo, were equal to the might of Britain, France and Holland.

Conflicts over trade were the most likely causes of trouble. Louis XIV began a trade war with Britain, by raising import taxes. Britain retaliated and it was the Bretons and in particular the area around Roscoff that suffered. Its textile industry was destroyed and by the time France realised in 1713 that Louis XIV had acted foolishly, many industries in Brittany had been ruined. But the Roscoff merchants continued to prosper by smuggling wine and brandy until 1792 and the French Revolution. In the wars that followed the Revolution the French navy – and the ships of the Breton corsairs – were destroyed.

Descent into poverty

In spite of the fertile land, the majority of the people were desperately poor. They tilled the soil, produced excellent vegetables - and ate gruel. The price of land was beyond the reach of labourers and any owner of a sizeable piece of land enjoyed an endless source of income. Even today, farmers in the Roscoff area rent much of the land they work.

The population of Roscoff and Saint-Pol-de-Leon was unusually high for a rural area. From 1897 to 1914, for example, there were 270 people per square kilometre – compared to 163 in Plougastel, 188 in Pont l'Abbé and 122 in Lesardrieux.

Merchants were bleeding the farmers, buying entire crops before they were harvested and not paying for them until the end of the season and often withholding money if they considered the quality of the vegetables to be poor.

A divided society evolved. There were rich landowners and desperately poor labourers. The labourers would seek to be hired by the day. They would gather at the Place du Parvis in Saint-Pol – hence the Breton word *placenner* for those who were reduced to seeking employment in this way. These workers were the most poorly paid in the whole of Brittany. At the end of the 19th century they received 1.19 francs (about £2.70 at present day value). This compared with 2.04 francs in the rest of north Finistère and an average for Brittany of 2.57 francs. The work was seasonable – once the seeds were sown there was little to do until the harvest. Life was a misery.

It was not surprising that there was no shortage of volunteers prepared to cross the sea, spend the winter living in damp and freezing warehouses and condemned buildings and go from door to door in the cold and the rain to sell painfully heavy loads of onions carried on a stick on the shoulder. They needed very little persuasion to follow in the footsteps of Henri Olivier.

Favourable conditions in Britain

Poverty ensured a supply of workers. But in Britain conditions were beginning to favour such a trade. The product was excellent – a hard, red, mild onion, carefully dried in the warm sun and mild breezes of Brittany. It keeps better than any other onion – a vital factor for a company of Johnnies bringing, perhaps, 20 tons of onions that might take months to sell. Furthermore, the housewife would expect her string of onions to last a further month or two in her kitchen without rotting.

In Britain, the Industrial Revolution was forging ahead faster than anywhere in Europe. The British government had little sympathy with the plight of small farmers and the choice for them was to starve or find work in factories, coalmines or ironworks. Between 1801 and 1901 the population of Britain increased from 16 million to 45 million. In the same period the rural population dropped by 29 per cent. Rural Britain could no longer feed its urban population.

Cheap corn from the United States was swamping the markets of Britain and Europe, and Britain was becoming increasingly dependent on imported food. Industrial Britain was producing more and more and to ensure a market for these products it had to open its ports to foreign imports, mostly food.

Ten years after Henri Olivier had made his first journey supporters of free trade were gathering momentum in Britain. In 1842 import tax was slashed. Crop failures in Britain and Ireland led to further relaxation of imports and the Corn Laws were repealed in 1846. Laws stipulating ships from which countries could dock in British ports were no longer applied and in 1853 the powers of the port authorities were reduced. As entry into Britain became increasingly easier so the number of Johnnies increased.

Once they arrived, the Bretons found they had an eager market for their onions. The onion was no one's staple diet. Nor was it exactly a luxury. Nevertheless, it was something tasty for the wife of a steelworker, quarryman or miner to put in her husband's lunchbox. Versatile, it could be used with cheese in a sandwich, it could be fried, it made the stew tastier. It was equally welcome to the wives of farmers. The onions of the Johnnies were better than anything the farmer could grow in his field or the industrial worker in his allotment.

Getting ready for the new season

Before departing for Britain the Johnnies had to ensure they had a good supply of onions. They would grow some, and many more were bought on credit from neighbouring farmers during the months of May and June. In the early period – prior to 1914 – the Johnnies operated in companies of between 15 and 30 men. In 1902, according to the geographer and social historian Camille Vallaux, 72 companies sailed for Britain. The largest consisted of 42 men.

A number of men would invest jointly in the coming season, pledging so many tons of onions that they themselves had grown, or sums of money to buy onions to sell in Britain. Deals were struck over bottles of wine in the Ty Pierre or Chez Janie or one of the many cafés on Roscoff's old port. These were recorded in a "register" kept in the café.

Next they had to hire workers. Again these deals were struck in the cafés and recorded in the "register". A wage was agreed and the certainty of a place to sleep – usually a corner of the warehouse alongside the sacks of onions. All food was inclusive and sometimes a quantity of tobacco. For the stringers two pints of beer a day was part of the deal. Up to World War II it was not unusual to have children working in every company. It was the responsibility of the "boss" or Ar Master to ensure they had clothes, were treated fairly and not abused in any way. When Jean-Marie Cueff went to work for the first time in Bryn-mawr in South Wales he was nine years of age and his pay was his keep, a year's rent for his unmarried mother and a pair of boots. One fewer mouth to feed back home in Brittany meant a lot.

Traditionally, the Johnnies would sail from the old port of Roscoff on the day after the Fête – or Pardon – of Sainte Barbe. This is celebrated on the third Sunday and Monday in July. The Pardons are unique to Brittany, possibly an ancient ritual to do with veneration of the dead and worship of the saints – usually Celtic saints. They include a procession with banners from churches, followed by mass and an afternoon of eating and drinking.

On the day of the Pardon of Sainte Barbe the onion sellers and their families would proceed to the tiny white-washed chapel of Sainte Barbe which stands on a hillock on the eastern end of the old port of Roscoff. The deep-water harbour of Roscoff, main port of Brittany Ferries, is to the east, or more precisely, to the south of the chapel. The day of the Pardon was significant in the lives of the Johnnies and their families. It was the day they prayed together to Sainte Barbe for the same return of the onion sellers. In the old days there would be a bonfire after vespers, but like so many customs it has died. Olivier Bertevas, an old Johnny who throughout his life had sold onions in Cardiff, told me how the priest had stopped the celebrations from spilling over to the Monday. Jean-Marie Cueff told me that he always went to the chapel a few days before he sailed to put money in the collection box, to ensure his safe return.

On the day after the Pardon the old port was buzzing. Horse drawn carts would wind their way through the wispy morning mist from the villages of Cleder and Plouescat to Saint-Pol and down to the port. These were the farmers bringing their sacks of onions to be loaded into the sailing boats on the quay. Other carts carried the onion sellers and their wives. The children sat on the trunks of the men who would soon be leaving for Britain.

The men talked and laughed loudly thumping knees and shoulders enthusiastically. The women responded in words of one syllable unable, or unwilling, to share the boisterous enthusiasm of the departing Johnnies.

When they arrived in Roscoff the wives would go to the shops to make a last minute purchase or light a candle and offer a prayer in the Chapel of Sainte Barbe. The men gathered in the cafés to talk and drink. It was a day for drinking and talking – a day to prepare the apprentices, the *nevezhanted*, for the fun and customs, the short days and long damp nights in a new country.

While the Johnnies drank and talked the ships were loaded. Sacks of onions were pushed down the slide (la glissière) to the schooners and the great dundees, small ships with two masts the one to the fore larger that the one at the rear. Ships with Breton names like *Kenavo, Araok, Sainte Anne* and *Jeanne*. In July and August of 1928 and 1929 it was not unusual to see a dozen ships sailing with very tide.

The Departure

After the farewells those left behind would walk to the Chapel of Sainte Barbe and as the sailing boats slid out of the old harbour between the chapel and an islet known as Enez Ty Saozon (The Isle of the house of the English) the wives sang their song in paise of Sainte Barbe – *Kanomp gant joa meuleudi da Santez Barba* (Joyfully we sing the praises of Sainte Barbe). Respectfully, the ships would lower their flags to the Patron Saint of the Onion Sellers and the men would take up the song. Then together they sang the anthem of the men of Roscoff – *N'eus par e Breiz Izel da baotred Rosko ...* ('Nowhere in Lower Brittany are there men like the boys of Roscoff ...') In later years the steamers would cut the engines, to hear the women sing in honour of Sainte Barbe. In no time the two groups would be out of each other's sight, and in many cases would not be re-united until Christmas.

Nearly every old Johnny I have spoken to had at some time or other made the crossing under sail. The last time a sailing boat brought onions over to Britain was in 1952 – it was the *Mat Atao* now used as a training ship in the naval school in Paimpol.

It was without doubt quite an adventure. Olivier Creignou told me of a journey to Aberdeen that took three weeks. "For three days there was not a breath of wind. A week went by and we were still bobbing about within sight of Roscoff. Then a wind picked up and we made swift progress. Then as we were in sight of Scotland we ran into a gale and we ended up almost in sight of Norway. And I was sick all the way."

Some of the Johnnies were sailors as well as farmers and farm workers. Others disliked the sea. Marie Le Goff went with her husband to sell onions in Llanelli after the Great War. "I used to be sick all the way, and when we crossed in a sailing boat from Roscoff to

Swansea it could take a week if the wind was not right." She made the journey every year – apart from the years of World War II – from the end of the Great War until 1979. She was a widow long before that but continued to make the journey with her daughter and son-in-law.

The steamers made the crossing a less chancy affair. In the days of sail many of the Johnnies crossed with their onions, sleeping in the hold and assisting the sailors. The enforcing of the Aliens Act of 1905 limited the number of onion sellers who could cross on boats destined for ports that were not established ports of immigration. (I shall deal with this in a later chapter.) Many of the bosses, and a few employees, would cross ahead of the men and the onions – to ensure they had a store and cut the reeds for stringing.

After World War II it was usual for the onion men to take the train to Cherbourg or Calais, cross over by ferry and then take a train again to their final destination.

In 1972, the Kerisnel, the first of the Brittany Ferries boats crossed from Roscoff's new deep-water port. It was the beginning of *"roll on roll off"* and three lorries full of onions were on that first historic crossing. It was accepted that a quantity of vegetables would be ruined by the loading and unloading at the ports. Now they were loaded on to a lorry and not unloaded again until they arrived at their destination. Once again, as on Henri Olivier's first journey, the men crossed over on the same boat as their onions. But things had moved on a long way since then.

The Agent

As the trade of the Johnnies developed the agents became an important part of their organisation. The name Le Guerch is one known to generations of onion sellers. It is probable that a portrayal of Marie Johnniguet in Yves-Marie Rudel's novel *Johnny de Roscoff* was based on one of the women in that formidable family.

"The cheerful band raise their glasses to Marie Johnniguet who weaves her way amongst the tables, exchanging a few words here and there. She would organise the journeys on behalf of the Johnnies, following the progress and tribulations of her customers by letter, some of them about to embark on a journey that will take them to the furthest corners of Britain. She would arrange for fresh supplies to be sent to her customers during the selling season."

The last of the Le Guerch family is Madeleine, living a comfortable retirement in – appropriately – *Rue des Johnnies in Roscoff*. Her grandmother's house was sold in 1936 and bought by the port to be used by the customs. At the age of 21, a few years after the end of World War II, she followed in the footsteps of her great-grandmother, grandmother and mother and became one of the Johnnies' agents.

Walking around Roscoff with Madeleine is like tasting a slice of the town's social history. "Here was my father's warehouse ... my mother's café ... this café was built by my grandfather ..." Take her into any one of the town's many restaurants and she gets a warm welcome from the owner, or the chef or a young waiter. "His father was a Johnny, one of my customers ... his father was a farmer, I would buy onions from him for my Johnnies ..."

She gave me her family background: "My father and grandfather were vegetable exporters and my mother had a café next to the vegetable warehouse. The Johnnies would come to my father and ask for advice about the customs formalities. Most of them were farm labourers or small peasant farmers and such matters worried them. My father would say, 'Go to the café and ask my wife, she will help you.' And she would make the arrangements for them.

"Another of their worries was to make sure they had somewhere to live and store their onions when they arrived at their destination. They would stay in the poor areas, old warehouses in the docks or inner city areas. It was unlikely that anyone else would have taken possession or rented the building, but it was possible that it had been knocked down for re-development. So I would write letters on their behalf to the owner to make sure that all was well."

It was a fact that many of them took the keys to the stores home with them to Brittany at the end of the season. Their condition was such that no one was likely to need these buildings. "Peta Claude" Corre, a little onion seller who used to go to Glasgow, told me that he did this regularly in his latter years.

Many of the onion men would write regularly to Madeleine Le Guerch when they were in Britain. "I would get a letter every week from Jean-Marie Cueff in Cardiff. Every one would begin 'It's Sunday once again and it is my duty to write to you ...' Writing a letter was hard work for many of them. After all, Cueff had spent very little time in school." He had started work as a Johnny at the age of nine. Before World War II this was not uncommon. The French authorities were more than happy to let children go to work in "England". The view was that they would learn English and this would be more useful to them than any formal schooling. Certainly, many of them profited from being multi-lingual after the fall of France at the beginning of World War II. Many, after being taken prisoner, were forced to work as translators by the Germans. It was the least unpleasant job they might have to do for their captors.

"I would also charter ships for Johnnies," continued Madeleine. "The period immediately after World War II was particularly difficult as so many French ships had been destroyed. I would charter anything I could find, sailing boats – the *Mat Atao*, was one of them – steamers, anything. I would charter ships from a Dutch company, large ships, and those would be used for the longer journeys to Scotland and the north of England. Smaller ships would be used for the south coast of England and for Wales."

She saw a great change when *Brittany Ferries* was established in 1972. "From then on I was hiring lorries instead of chartering ships."

The Johnnies were, invariably, multi-lingual. Their wives, in many cases, spoke only Breton. The wife of Joseph Olivier, an old onion Johnny from Santec, would always insist on speaking to Madeleine's mother. "She would come to the café and ask me 'Where's your mother?' I might have to say that she was away for the day. The she would say, 'But I can't talk to you, you can't speak Breton to me!' Then we would agree – she would speak Breton and I would reply in French."

I knew Joseph Oliver's son, Michel, also a former Johnny and he told me his younger sister would speak no Breton. Quite a language shift in one generation!

Chapter 2

Johnny Onions in Britain

The Companies

The head of every company was The Boss or The Master. And since the onion sellers absorbed many English words into their Breton – *Ar Master.* Where two or three bosses had invested equally in the company, there could be more than one Master. But usually, the investment of one – whether in money or onions - would be greater than that of the others. That person would then be the Boss or Master.

It was his responsibility to arbitrate when there were arguments. He would be responsible for ensuring that there was a store for the onions and a place for his men to sleep. He would arrange for fresh supplies of onions to be sent over as required during the selling season. He would decide where they would sell, the price and collect and count the money when the sellers returned in the evening. And, particularly in the period before World War I, it was his responsibility to take the money back safely to Brittany. After World War II, and generally in the period between the wars, the money was paid into a bank in Britain and then transferred to the onion sellers' bank in Brittany – usually the Banque de Bretagne in Saint-Pol-de-Leon. The members of the company were paid at a dinner, traditionally arranged in one of the restaurants of Roscoff or Saint-Pol, after they had returned.

The Master was expected to set a good example - the first out of bed in the morning. He had to ensure there were no problems with the authorities and that relations with the police were good. Under the Aliens Order, 1920, every Johnny had to take his registration card, as soon as he arrived at his destination, to be signed at the Police Station. Generally, the Johnnies were on good terms with the police. A policeman on duty was always welcome to drop in at the warehouse for a cup of tea and a chat in the evenings. Since the onion men travelled about quite a lot there was always a chance that they might have bits of information of interest to the police. "I wouldn't go so far as to say that I liked the 'bobby' , but I would rather talk to him than the *gendarme* any day," the late Michel Olivier, an onion seller whose base was in Newcastle Emlyn, once told me.

The Master was also expected to take good care of the younger members of the company. It was not unusual, in the inter-war years for children of nine and ten to be out selling onions in the atreets. Most of the older Johnnies I interviewed had started at the age of twelve. In 1896 a series of articles about the Johnnies appeared in the Plymouth *Western Daily Mercury*. These articles alerted the NSPCC to the fact that very young children were coming over from Brittany to live in rough conditions in warehouses and going out on the streets selling onions. There was an inquiry but the NSPCC concluded that the little Onion Johnnies were adequately looked after and better fed than most children of a similar age in Plymouth even if they were made to work hard. I never heard of any young Johnny being ill-treated but there must have been some tough bosses around. François Keriven – I mention two Johnnies of that name later, this was the older of the two – told me of the trouble his boss had to get him out selling. There were bribes of bits of chocolate and threats of a hiding. "I never wanted to leave the store," he said.

Claude Corre, as a boy in Glasgow had required an operation, and he told me how his father had been rebuked by a surgeon for allowing him to live in such conditions.

When Thérèse Prigent, was about nine or ten she would go over with her parents to Llanelli. "I was never made to work, just be there with the family," she said. "But I remember playing in the docks one day and found a boy of my age asleep alongside a pile of onions. I knew him well although he was with another company. I woke him up and he started crying saying that he would be thrashed if he returned to the store without selling all the onions. I told him, 'come to see my mother'. My mother took pity on him and bought all his onions. This arrangement went for weeks!"

But it has been said that "a good cry and a good lie was part of the little Johnny's stock in trade".

The Stringer

The onions were shipped to Britain in sacks and the stringing was done in the store. Stringing was a vital skill. Presentation was considered to be very important. The dozen or fifteen onion of the string had to appear as attractive as possible to the buyer.

After arriving at the start of a new season the first thing that had to be done was to go off and cut reeds, from the marshes or the side of the mountain. Often water would seep out over the floor from the pile of reeds, adding to the dampness and misery of the store.

From early morning until evening the stringer would be on his feet, shoulders hunched as he worked away. Eight or ten reeds, and a piece of raffia was used to attach the onions by the withered stem – or 'tail' - to the reeds to make the string. It was important that the onions had a good 'tail' otherwise they were impossible to attach to the reeds. A large onion was placed at the bottom to anchor the string and then smaller onions with their sizes getting bigger and bigger towards the top. The raffia in one complete piece was wound around the 'tails' and the reeds from the bottom to the top. Then a second string was done and the two tied together at the top to make a bunch - or *pakaat* in Breton. Each bunch is sold for about £5 these days.

Like an old woman picking up her knitting these men would get on with their work, talking amongst themselves or singing an old Breton ballad, their backs bent, shoulders hunched and feet firmly on the ground. Traditionally, the stringer was also the cook. Sometimes the boss's wife came over as part of the company and she would cook, keep the place clean and tidy and do some stringing.

The stringer was mostly confined to the base and apart from going to the pub in the evening he rarely left the stores. It was agreed that every stringer was entitled to two pints of beer a day, in addition to his wage, food and bed. I have been told that some would forfeit the beer and take the money at the end of the season. They were rare creatures and I never met one who admitted to receiving money in preference to the beer!

There was a lot of respect for a good stringer and even in very recent times he was much in demand. Patrick Mevel, the last of the bosses who still has a 'company' coming to Britain every year, spoke with great affection of his grandfather who had taught him to string. "He was one the finest," he says of the man who came with him to Cardiff for the first time in 1980.

The Seller

The sellers were out and about in all weather, knocking on doors, all day and everyday – except Sunday. *Chiner* (pronounced sheener) was the word they used for this door-to-door selling. The seller was expected to be up at six, to have eaten his breakfast, got his load ready and be knocking doors by the time the husbands were off to work and the children to school. Before 1914 the sellers would carry their onions on a stick or *ar vaz* – the Breton word for a stick or cudgel. A stick with a number of notches at both ends so the strings of onions would not slip off. On this stick they would carry 10 or 12 kilograms. "I would start out with twenty bunches on the stick – that was more than a 100 pounds," François Gueguen an old onion seller from Roscoff who had spent more than half his working life selling onions in Kendall, Middlesborough and Durham, told me. "I would just be thankful that the load would get lighter as the day went on." Some of the sellers, if they were going out into the country and the villages would use a wheelbarrow or a handcart.

Around 1921 the bicycle, with their handlebars, became the peferred method of carrying the onions around. Wheeling a bike it was possible to carry between 75 and 100 kilograms – the Johnnies could go further – and while it was not a good idea to try to ride such a heavily laden bicycle it could always be ridden back to the store at the end of the day. These bicycles were often adapted to increase the number of bunches that could be carried on them. A former onion seller who used to go to Scotland once showed me a spectacular piece of workmanship. A blacksmith had welded a rod of iron along the handlebars increasing its width by at least a foot. Another rod had been attached behind the seat. Usually pieces of wood would cover the wheels so that the spokes did not ruin the onions. This Johnny had come up with another idea – pieces of fishing net covered the bottom part of the wheels. When I was helping to establish *La Maison des Johnnies* – the onion sellers' museum - in Roscoff I tried to persuade him to lend his unique bicycle to the museum. So far I have had no success!

In the 1920s many of the masters bought vans so they could go even further a-field to sell their onions. Jean-Marie Roignant claimed that he used to drive an old Ford van with wooden wheels and three gears – two for going forward and a reverse – around Anglesey in this period. He would have been 14 or 15 at the time. He was a small man when I knew him – he must have looked suspiciously small at the age of 14! In his own words he was *comme trois pommes* – like three apples, the French equivalent of knee-high to a grasshopper and the children he was sometimes allowed to play with in North Wales, were very surprised when they saw him behind the steering-wheel of this van.

The stick, *ar vaz*, had a new lease of life as the vans became more popular. A Johnny could be dropped off at a village or small town with a load of onions on the stick and picked up in the evening. Patrick Mevel, in Cardiff, goes a step further. He drops his sellers in the towns and villages with a bicycle and onions – even though the bikes never seem to have chains or tyres. At least he has great respect for tradition! Sometimes they will travel to North Wales or far into the West of England dropping off their sellers and their bicycles as they go. And then pick them all up on the way back at night. In the 1920s it was common for onion sellers to take their bikes and onions on buses and trains.

The onion sellers were generally considered to be cheerful, with a ready smile – and persistent. In parts of England they were referred to as the bell-breakers. If the housewife refused to answer the door when they rang, they would pull on the bell until it broke. Once she came to the door she would succumb to the Gallic charm. If she slammed the door in his face, it was said that he would come knocking at the window, or the back door!

I heard of one Johnny in Caerphilly who made his rounds on a Friday morning, following the milkman down the road. Friday was the morning the milkman collected his money, and when the women answered his knock, there was the onion man standing, smiling, behind him!

In the years after World War II their numbers gradually dwindled and there was no longer any need for high-pressure sales. Nowadays, an onion man is such a rarity that he will stand outside the market or in the centre of town and wait for the buyers to come to him.

Chapter 3

Memories of the Johnnies

The "Welsh" Johnnies

A novice – or *nevezhant* - had a lot to learn. In the days of pre-decimal money, sixpence, shilling, half-a-crown, ten bob, were very strange to the onion men, and very complicated. Then they had to learn the language.

"I was told to say 'Would you like some onions, please?' Very often I didn't understand the reply, but I was told always to say 'Please' and 'Thank you'," said Olivier Olivier who used to sell onions in Haverfordwest, Pembrokeshire.

"Other phrases I learnt were 'May I have a drink of water – or a piece of bread – please?'"

Olivier would describe how he walked the streets of Haverfordwest every day. It's a small, old town with many hills, and the stick with its load of onions would rub into his shoulder. "I'd had enough of all the walking," he said, "And, of course, I was calling on the same people many times in the same week. And they would tell me, 'Do you think we never eat anything except onions? Do you think we get up at three o'clock in the morning to eat an onion?' My boss had a horse and cart and he used to go around the country to sell his onions. In the end I told him that if he didn't have a bike for me the following season I would go and work for someone else. And the next autumn I had my bike. On my first day I went off out into the country and I sold all my onions in no time at all.

"The next day when I got back to the store the boss was waiting for me and from the look on his face I thought to myself, 'Oh, dear, this is trouble'. And he told me, 'You have been out in the country and you have been selling onions to my customers!' After that I was a lot more careful."

When Olivier first came over it was by sailing boat. The boat sailed into Milford Haven and was pulled up to Haverfordwest by a tug. The warehouse was next door to the Bristol Trader public house.

* * *

A few days before Christmas, 2000, I heard that another of the Olivier family had died. Michel Olivier, from Santec, was in his mid-fifties and the last of the fluently Welsh speaking Johnnies – a real *Shoni Winwns*. He had finally lost his battle against cancer.

He came to sell onions with his father, Joseph, in Newcastle Emlyn when he was 15 which would have been about 1960, and they returned for the last time in 1975. He had been over for 15 seasons and spoke Welsh fluently and claimed that he could not speak a word of English.

"The first time I came over my father took me in the van and left me with a bike in St David's while he went off somewhere else to sell," he said. "He had written the name of the place where I was supposed to meet him in the evening on my hand.

"But because of the sweat and the rubbing of handlebars the name had gone. I had sold all my onions and there was no sign of my father. Someone told me that he had seen a van going back and fore. In the end I decided to find my way back to the store.

"Walking and cycling – cycling in the dark with no lights on the bike was a serious offence in the country in those days – so I had to be very careful when I did get on the bike. Through Fishguard, Eglwyswrw, Boncath, Aber-cuch – I got to Newcastle Emlyn about five in the morning. It was a long journey.

"Then I had to start work again at six. I didn't get much sympathy from my father although he had been driving around for hours looking for me. He had gone to the police station and someone had reported seeing a youngster with a bike crying in St David's.

"I would quarrel a lot with him and I would tell him that I wanted to go home to Mam. All he would say was 'Go on then' and offer me my passport. He knew very well that I would not be able to find my way back to Brittany."

Later, he would drive on his own around the farms of northern Pembrokeshire and Ceredigion. "Sometimes the farm would be up a track a mile from the road and I would have as many as eight gates to open and close on the way to the farm and the way back. It was a lot of starting and stopping to get to one farm. And sometimes there would be no answer when I got there. But if I saw the curtains twitch I would jump into the van, drive away slowly and leave the first gate open. Farmers were very annoyed if you left their gates open, because their animals would get out on to the road or into the crops. If the housewife didn't come running after me that day she would always come out to complain to me the next time I called! Then I usually managed to make a sale!

"I remember an occasion when one of the other Johnnies in the company had sold a string of rotten onions to a farmer near Newcastle Emlyn. The next time the farmer saw the Johnny he complained and the Johnny said 'I'm afraid you'll have to talk to the boss'. A week later the same farmer saw another Johnny and complained to him. Again he was told that he would have to 'see the boss'. This went on for a few weeks. One night we were all having a pint in the Ivy Bush in Newcastle Emlyn when in walked the farmer and he stood in front of us and he said, 'Right then, you beggars, which one of you is the boss?'"

Pubs were very popular with the Johnnies. Drinking was part of life in Brittany, but in Britain, pubs offered warmth and a little comfort away from the cold misery of the warehouses and tramping the streets in wind, rain and snow. "Every Sunday we would drink in the Nag's Head in Aber-cuch," said Michel. He usually referred to it as *Tafarn llygoden* ('the pub of the rat'). There was, what looked like, a huge stuffed rat in a glass box in the pub. A former owner had caught this massive rodent eating the cabbages in his garden. It was believed to be a South American coipou, a fairly harmless creature that had probably stowed away on a boat that had sailed into Cardigan.

The three counties – Ceredigion, Carmarthenshire and Pembrokeshire – border each other near Aber-cuch and of the three Pembrokeshire was the first to open its pubs on Sundays. Aber-cuch – and the Nag's Head – was in Pembrokeshire.

Michel, his father, and the other sellers were based in a store in Cwrt Coed, a farm owned by a colourful character called Ben James. "Whenever we asked him for anything he always said 'no', but in the end he always agreed to whatever we asked. He would drive to Cardigan for petrol if he thought it was a half-penny cheaper there – and spend more than he saved driving there and back!"

Michel was recorded a number of times for *Radio Cymru*, and twice for S4C, the Welsh Language Channel. He had agreed a few years ago to come over once more to Newcastle Emlyn for a Welsh television feature. Then, without explanation, he refused. When I went to talk to face-to-face some months later he explained that he had cancer. He died a few weeks before Christmas 2000.

He had been married for a while – a girl from Paris, someone told me. Not every woman could cope with being the wife of a Johnny and a small farmer. After the death of his parents he lived on in the family farm in Mecheroux (Mechou Rouz in Breton) growing carrots and cauliflowers and some onions and garlic. His brother has an electricity business in Santec and his greatest pleasure towards the end of his life was to go fishing for mackerel in his bother's boat around Île de Siek. Since much of the land he farmed was rented when he first became ill he gave up running his own farm and went to work for another farmer.

* * *

The Johnnies from Santec and its neighbouring village Dossen traditionally went to hawk their onions in Wales. Olivier Olivier, whose home was behind the old lighthouse on the seafront at Roscoff, was an exception. But he, too, had connections with the Santec and Dossen area. Joseph Oliver, father of Michel, from Mecheroux a hamlet half way between the two villages, was his cousin.

The brothers Autret, who went to Porthmadog, live on the outskirts of Santec. So to do the Gallou family who went Port Talbot and Aberavon. The late Yves Gallou owned a house in Santec which he had named Aberavon, and a house in Aberavon he had named Santec. His widow, now re-married, keeps in touch with both.

And, of course, there was Joseph Olivier. He spoke Welsh as fluently as any Welshman. Olivier Bertevas, one of the last of the old school of Cardiff Johnnies, told me about him. "He never spoke English, I know because I had to translate for him when we were going through customs," said Bertevas. "But I'll tell you this, he sold a lot of onions."

I remember calling at his farm in Mecheroux. It was about two in the afternoon, and he and Michel were coming out after lunch. "Good afternoon, sir, how are you?" I said in Welsh. "Very well, my boy, where do you come from?" he replied in perfect Welsh. I asked if we could meet for chat. He replied, "By all means – but it will have to be on Sunday afternoon." This was not at all convenient for me, but he was polite – and very insistent. He and Michel were harvesting the cauliflowers and they got up early and worked until late. His only day off was Sunday. I had to agree and we arranged to meet in the Café

Tabac in Dossen at 5 pm the following Sunday.

I was at least half an hour late that Sunday. I walked into a crowded bar and as I looked around everyone stopped talking. I failed to see Joseph. There were two other rooms and I went into both and received the same auspicious reception. Silence – and still I could not see Joseph. I went back to the first bar, and this time a voice cut the silence. "Where have you been, my boy?" Joseph was in the corner, he was wearing a cap and I had not recognised him.

"And what time is this then?" he teased. He could have been a farmer from the heart of Ceredigion. "It's just turned 5.30," I lied lamely. "And what time did you say you would be here?" He was enjoying pulling my leg.

He was one of eight children, and it was no easy task to feed all those hungry mouths. "There was plenty of potatoes – and bread – a piece of bacon if we were lucky. If you didn't like bacon, it was tough luck. Occasionally, on a Sunday we would get fresh meat."

They were hard times when Joseph came to Newcastle Emlyn to sell onions with his father for the first time in 1931. He was twelve years of age. In those days the boat would sail into the Teifi estuary and up to the bridge at Cardigan. There the sacks of onion were loaded on to a lorry and taken to Newcastle Emlyn. For many years their base was Sussex Yard, Adpar, the part of Newcastle Emlyn which was in Cardiganshire – most of the town is in Camarthenshire. It was some years later that they moved to Cwrt Coed. Ben James was the owner of both the farm and the yard.

Joseph and his father had a van which they left permanently in Newcastle Emlyn. He recalled being taken to court for driving the van when he was sixteen years of age. "I was fined five shillings and my father was fined another five shillings for letting me." He even remembered the name of the policeman who had taken him to court – Simon Davies.

Evidently, they were selling onions over a wide area. When World War II began there were 14 onion sellers in Newcastle Emlyn. François Kergoat – Francis as he was known in the area - had a company of ten men in Lampeter. Joseph would go up as far as Aberaeron – but the town of Aberaeron was Kergoat's territory. After Kergoat retired Joseph and Michel extended their territory up to Tregaron and beyond. He also covered most of northern Pembrokeshire, the Welsh-speaking part at least. Once a month Joseph would travel down to

Maenclochog in the heart of the Preseli Mountains where he would meet his cousin, Olivier Olivier, who would come up from Haverfordwest and they would have a few pints together.

When the war broke Joseph had to return to France. But as soon as France fell he returned to Britain with many other Bretons to join the Free French in response to Charles de Gaulle's request. He spent the war sailing between Lisbon, Freetown and Greenock. In 1948 he was back selling onions in Newcastle Emlyn.

I remember talking to him in 1979 when he still longed to see his Welsh friends in the pubs of Newcastle Emlyn. He had been made welcome by the Welsh and been given clothes, food and an open door at all times. When he needed money to pay the import duty on the onions it was sometimes lent to him by one of the pubs, or by Ben James. "I would always repay the loan by the end of the first week, but I have a lot to be thankful for," said Joseph. "And the people in Cwrt Coed, they were the best people I have ever known. And I am greatly indebted to Ben James."

English people moved in and settled in the Teifi valley after the war and Joseph found that he did not get on so well with them. "I remember they couldn't pronounce the names of places like Crymych and Aber-cuch – they would say Crimick and Aber-kick. But I regret very much stopping coming to Wales to sell onions, the Welsh people were so nice."

He would bring over 20 tons of onions at the beginning of the season. His wife would arrange to send over another 20 tons in November and then they would bring over another 20 tons when they returned after Christmas. "Sometimes I would go into the heart of the Preseli mountains in Pembrokeshire and walk to the farms around the mountain and the van would pick me up in the evening. I often walked a mile from the road to the farm and another mile back to the farm before going on to the next farm – I needed to make a good sale at those farms to make all that walking worth while. I used to sell strings in three sizes and fair play to the women on those farms, they always bought the biggest." Years later I discovered that Patrick Mevel, who still comes to Cardiff, has strings of different sizes, £5 ones for Wales and bigger ones he sells for £8 to take to Bristol.

On one occasion I read Joseph a poem by the celebrated Welsh poet and farmer Isfoel (David Jones). Its title was *Shoni Winwns – adeg rhyfel* (Johnny Onions – war time).

Saint Pol-de-Leon with the Cathedral in the centre of the picture – a sign of old wealth.

One of the houses in Roskogoz (Old Roscoff) – another sign of a glorious past.

The Corsairs. An aspect of Roscoff and Brittany's power and colourful past.

Gathering seaweed on a beach near Plouescat – seaweed is the traditional fertilizer for the Roscoff onions.

Postcard of a boy with onions.
The tradition of stringing onions and
vegetables goes back a long way.

A field of artichokes – the fertile fields
of the Johnnies.

A beach opposite Île de Siek.

An old photograph of the Pardon of Sainte Barbe. The first Johnnies would be sailing for Britain after the Pardon on the third Monday in July.

Sacks of onions ready for loading on the old quay in Roscoff.

Unloading the carts on the old quay.

Loading the sailing boat.

The empty carts and the boat preparing to sail.

A familar scene in the old port of Roscoff at the end of July and August.

The Chapel of Sainte Barbe. The women would come here to pray as the onion men sailed away.

Madeleine Le Guerch, the last in a line of agents for the Johnnies.

Jeanne Le Guerch, agent in an earlier era – she was Madeleine's grandmother.

Outside the café of the Le Guerch family. Madeleine Le Guerch, who became the last of the agents is the little girl in the front row. This was one of the cafés where the Masters and the Johnnies would agree terms and their contracts entered in a register kept at the café.

A stringer at work.

The wife of a Johnny stringing onions –
Jeanne Gallou in Cwmavon, southern Wales.

A string of shallots and a string of onions
beautifully tied. An attractive string of
onions would always sell.

An unknown Johnny in Monmouthshire
between the wars – his photograph taken
in a studio.

Johnnies in a street in Cardiff Docks in the first decade of the 20th century. Companies were large in those days.

La Roscovite, *back in Roscoff.*

Jean Berthou of Cleder. He started selling onions in Aberdeen before the Great War. He returned to Roscoff in August 1914 after the outbreak of war, a jouney that took a month by sea. When this photograph was taken in 1979 he was over 80 years of age. Here he is collecting onion seeds to sow in two years time.

Paotred Rosko e Leith – the boys of Roscoff in Leith, Edinburgh. Companies became smaller after the Great War – but the number of companies increased.

Claude Tanguy as a young man in Leith.   *Caude Tanguy in middle aged.*

Claude Tanguy, as an old man in Roscoff.

André Quémenér selling onions in Scotland after the Second World War.

A company of Johnnies in Scotland after the Great War.

43

Madame Roignant, wife of Jean-Marie Roignant, with her daughter Françoise, in Perth after the Second World War. Note the hand scale they are holding. After the Second World War every onion seller was obliged by law to have a scale in their possession at all times.

Fançoise Roignant with her uncle, again in Perth.

'Peta' Claude Corre selling onions in Glasgow for the first time. His father is on the right and a customer in the centre.

'Peta' Claude, guest of honour at a Burns Night in Glasgow. He said that he translated one of Burns's famous songs, Ye banks and braes, to Breton and had sung it that night!

44

*'Peta' Claude an old man in Roscoff in
1979 – he died a few years later.*

*Marie Le Goff's family in Santec. From the left: Sebastien Prigent (in his Breton hat),
Thérèse Prigent, Marie le Goff – Thérèse's mother – and Marie-Josie, daughter of
Thérèse and Sebastien. Marie Le Goff came to sell onions in Llanelli, South Wales, with
her parents after the Great War. She continued to come with her daughter Thérèse. They
were joined by Sebastien after he married Thérèse. Marie Josie never came to Llanelli to
sell onions but she spent two terms of every school year in the Catholic Primary School
in Llanelli. The author is on the right.*

Marie Le Goff in her traditional Breton costume.

Jean-Marie Cueff (left) and Olivier Bertevas outside their shop in Bute Street, Cardiff, in 1978. The shop has gone – and sadly so have they.

Olivier Bertevas in The Hayes, in the centre of Cardiff. There is always an onion seller at this spot every Saturday morning during the winter months.

Jean-Marie Cueff loading his bike.

Pierre Guivac'h who sold onions in Swansea, Newcastle and in Scotland. This picture was taken at his home in Dossen after he had retired to grow carrots on his small farm.

Jean-Marie Guivac'h – Pierre's brother – who sold onions in Newcastle Emlyn, Carmarthen, Aberystwyth, and in Scotland.

Michel Olivier (left) and his father, Joseph, who came to Newcastle Emlyn. Both spoke Welsh fluently – and no English! This photograph was taken in 1980 outside their farmhouse in Mecheroux, near Santec.

Michel Olivierbeing interviewed
by the author for a Radio Cymru
programme in 1989.

Claude Deridan with Jean Guivac'h and
Yves Hervé, a Breton who was the
manager of the Prince of Wales
in Cricieth.

Claude Deridan's company in Porthmadog (north Wales) in the 1950s. Deridan began
selling onions in Wimbledon (London) after the Second World War and then came to
Porthmadog where his father had been before him.
He is standing in the back row with his wife.

The poet was worrying about the absence of Johnny during the war and wondering what had become of him. Then after the war Johnny turns up again.

Croeso mawr i'r newydd da,	*(Great welcome and good news,*
Penderfynu prynu rhaff	*A string of onions at the door*
A chael hwyl ar lyfu gên	*And the joy of licking lips*
Wedi gweld fod Shoni'n sâff.	*Knowing Johnny's safe once more.)*

He remembered the farm, Y Cilie, and would go there many times during the season and he remembered David Jones well, and 'the one with the ginger hair' (that would have been Alun Jones, another of the poets of this well-known family on the coast of Cardigan Bay.) He remembered that in Cardigan, on one occasion, Alun had given him a £5 note for a string of onions and Joseph, in error, had given him change of a £1. Neither had noticed the mistake. "I went to Cilie the following day to give him the right money," said Joseph. "We would go to Cilie sometimes to get reeds for stringing."

Years later, I remember talking to a student whose home was in Avranches but whose ancestors were onion sellers from Roscoff about the many Welsh poets who had praised the Johnnies. Often they would write in *cynghanedd*, the traditional Welsh strict metres, and he seemed flattered that the Welsh poets, in this classical form, had praised the humble onion sellers. Joseph was not in the least surprised, he knew many of these poets, farmers like himself.

* * *

Joseph – like his son Michel – claimed that he could not speak English and others assured me that this was true. Breton was the language of the stores and English – or in the case of many parts of Wales – Welsh was the language of life outside the stores.

Some years ago I was given a cutting from the South Wales Daily Post & Cambrian Daily Leader, November 17, 1930. This is what appeared:

BRETON ONION SELLER IN THE SOUP
– Charles Floch, a Breton onion seller whose address was given as Llygad Vrych, Llanelli, was fined 20 shillings at Llanelli Police

Court for failing to have two obligatory lights in front of his motor lorry. He asked for the services of a Welsh interpreter. He said he could not understand English, but was able to understand Welsh.

One evening, a few winters, ago I was giving a lecture to Caerphilly Local History Society about the Johnnies. At the end of the evening an old man came to speak to me – I guess he was about 80 years of age. His family came from Pontrhydygroes in North Cardiganshire. He told me a story he had heard from his grandmother. His great grandmother was from Cornwall – many people from Cornwall had come to work in the lead mines of North Cardiganshire in the 19th century. The old man's story was that, one day, a Breton onion man arrived in the village. His grandmother spoke Welsh, his great grandmother spoke Cornish and the onion man spoke Breton and all three understood each other perfectly. Since the first onion man did not arrive in Britain until 1828, what does that make of the legend that the Cornish language died when Dolly Pentreath of Mousehole was buried in 1777?

Odette Keriven, who used to go with her parents to Hull, told me that as a child she had forgotten her French as a result of spending six months in England. Breton was the language of the store and English was the language of the street. "When I returned to Roscoff I had forgotten my French and the teachers and the other pupils would laugh at me," she told me.

* * *

Guillaume Le Duff – or Lom an Dukik – as he was known to his Breton speaking neighbours in Pen-ar-Prat, near Plouescat – had received a certain amount of education before he had gone to sell onions in Cardiff. He had gone to school when he was nine, but his mother died when he was 11 and his father had announced there would be no more school for him. He had, nevertheless, managed to get some schooling for the next two years. He was 15 when he went to sell onions for the first time in Cardiff. "What hope did children who started selling at the age of nine have?" he said. "When I went to Cardiff I would buy newspapers and in order to get some education I would read them in the evening after work. I could speak very little French in those days. French was the language in which I had been educated and I could read and write it quite well but I used to find it difficult to converse in the language until I went into the army in 1930. I spent most of my years in the army in Algeria.

"When I returned to sell onions in Cardiff after being in the army I remember going back to see a lady, she was French, who had been one of my customers. She praised my French and said it had improved a lot while I had been in the army. I never speak anything but Breton to my wife and my two sons are fluent in the language."

When he began selling onions in Cardiff he worked in a company of 20 sellers. "In those days the ship would sail up the West Dock as far as the old Spillers Mill. We would unload the onions ourselves; if the dockers did the work we'd have to pay them and that meant less profit. Then we'd go to the Butetown Tavern for a pint. We sold a lot of onions in pubs and someone would always buy us a half-pint before we left. Some of the Johnnies would go into pubs and raffle strings of onions – they had cloakoom tickets and sell a ticket for a few pennies to everyone in the pub, and then draw a ticket from the hat and the winner got the onions. I never did that.

"Eventually I went to work on my own. I worked like hell every day, Sundays too. In the end it was all too much for me. My wife was not in very good health and she worried a lot when I was away. I bought some more land and tried to make a better life for myself without going to Britain.

"I liked going to Cardiff and I made many good friends in Cardiff and Penarth. I still write to some of these people – they were very good to me. All except the police. I don't have happy memories of them. They once suspected me of murder and another time they questioned me in connection with a robbery. It's not a nice thing to happen to anyone, especially in a foreign country. The body of a woman was found in a field near Pen-y-lan, Cardiff, near the route I used every day. The police came to ask where I was on the day the woman had been killed. One policeman kept coming back and I became very frightened – my hair turned completely white and it remained like that until I returned to Brittany. I remember the policeman asking me whether I had blood on my clothes. I became so worried, I remember one day that I was crying while selling onions in Cardiff. On another occasion there had been a robbery in Whitchurch, a suburb of Cardiff, and the police came to interview me and ask where I had been at four o'clock the previous day."

But in the main his memories of Cardiff were relatively happy. "A black man once snatched a string of onions from my hand. I ran after him and he dropped the onions. On another occasion a man came up to me in a pub and said, 'You're a stranger here; we don't want your sort here.' Then two men who were sitting nearby said to him, 'You're the stranger here, get out and leave him alone.' I had plenty of friends in Cardiff."

He surprised me with his knowledge of Welsh. He did not know enough Welsh for us to converse in the language, but he would certainly have known enough to sell onions or to ask the way. It was sufficient for a basic level of communication. This was surprising as Cardiff had always been his base and when he was with a company they would always go towards the English-speaking areas of south-east Wales, even as far as Hereford and Symmonds Yat. "I could see that Welsh and Breton had a lot in common even though I didn't often come into contact with Welsh," he said.

He was a cultured man. When the war broke out in 1939 he had to return immediately to Brittany, was taken prisoner, and for part of the war was made to work as a translator on the Italian front, near Turin.

Before I left his farmhouse – pretty as a picture postcard with a sandy yard in front of it – he opened a small box. It contained letters from former customers in Cardiff and Penarth. Amongst them was a newspaper cutting from the *South Wales Echo* - the Cardiff evening paper – of January 16, 1973. It reported the death of his former friend and colleague.

"Vincent Cabioch died last week when boarding a ship at Roscoff, when he slipped on the gang plank and fell on the rocks between the vessel and the quay." The story went on to mention Cabioch's popularity – he had spent 35 seasons in Cardiff.

"If you see Olivier Bertevas in the next few days I would like you to give him this cutting. Vincent was his brother-in-law," said Lom. I promised, and indeed I did see Olivier a few days later and gave him the cutting.

It was the only time that I ever met Lom an Dukik. I called a number of times but there was never anyone at home. Sometimes, someone nearby said he was working in the fields, but the fields he owned, or rented, were in many directions and I never managed to find him. Also, since he lived on the edge of the Johnny Onions area, none of the Johnnies I would see regularly in Roscoff or Saint-Pol or

Santec knew anything about him.

* * *

Jean-Marie Prigent was a small man. He could have been a Welsh coal-miner, or someone who worked in the ironworks of the Monmouthshire valleys. He even talked like them, lively, voluble and his accent was South Wales Valleys English. "Do you know where the highest railway station in Britain can be found?" he asked me. I had no idea. I thought it was probably in Scotland, and anyhow, if I had known I was not going to spoil his fun. "Waunavon!" he said proudly. "I know, and I have been there." A friend who is an industrial historian and knew the area well confirmed that the little Prigent was right. It was the highest "ordinary" railway station in Britain. There are higher narrow gauge railway stations and a rack-and-pinion railway goes to the top of Snowdon, the highest mountain in Wales (and England, for that matter).

Jean-Marie Prigent – or Shamar Vihan as he was known among the Johnnies – lived close to the outskirts of Saint-Pol-de-Leon, and again not far from Santec. We met in a café known as the Rendez-vous des Amis. I am not sure whether it is still there, or perhaps its name has changed. He had started selling onions in Blaenavon – an area recently designated as a world heritage site such is its industrial archaeological significance. I think Shamar Vihan would have been pleased to know that had he lived to hear the news.

The first lesson he ever learnt was not to leave the onions on the stick in front of the house and go to knock at the back door. "The sheep would be there in a flash and they would nibble a piece off every onion on the string – never eat a whole onion, just spoil every onion on the string," he said. "I remember seeing sheep taking whole loaves out of women's shopping baskets in Broad Street – that was the main street in Blaenavon.

"Life was hard in those days. I can feel the *vaz* on my shoulder to this day. Sometimes the stick with its heavy load would rub my shoulder until it bled and by the time I got back that evening my shirt would be stuck in the dried blood. Mind you, life was hard in Wales those days too, bloody hard. Do you know where Pwll-du is? It's three miles over the mountain from Blaenavon. All you would find there was a pub, a farm and a row of houses. In 1923 I remember that everyone in Pwll-du worked in a limestone quarry, quarrying lime to build the Blaenavon steelworks with horses pulling the carts out. When I went there I would sell a string of onions in every house – nobody ever refused."

After 45 seasons it was no wonder that he could describe the area so accurately – and with such delight. "I would start at the bottom of Broad Street, sell a few strings in the butcher's shop, and then the pubs – I always did a good trade in the pubs." He listed his journeys in the years prior to his retirement, when he and a companion and a stringer came to Blaenavon. On Monday both would be selling in Abersychan and Tal-y-waun; Tuesday in Abertillery; Wednesday in Talybont-on-Usk and Brecon; Thursday in Aberfan, Treharris, Trelewis, Bedlinog, Fochriw and Rhymney; Friday, one selling in Tredegar and the other in Blaenavon; on Saturday, both of them and the stringer, would be selling in Tredegar.

The following week was as follows: Monday, Dowlais and Merthyr; Tuesday, Abertillery; Wednesday, one in Ebbw Vale and one in Aberbeeg; Thursday, Aberdare, Rhigos, Glyn-neath and Hirwaun; Friday, one in Blaenavon and the other in Brynmawr; Saturday, one in Blackwood and the other in Bryn-mawr. They would also make occasional visits to Gilwern, Llangynidr, Llanfoist and Abergavenny.

"But we never forced anyone to buy. We knew where to sell and who was lkely to buy," he said.

In 1994 I went looking for Shamar Vihan. I had been told that he was at a retirement home "near the super-markets at Saint-Pol". I arrived on a Sunday morning about 9.30 and told the woman at the reception that I was looking for an old Onion Johnny name of Jean-Marie Prigent. She looked very strangely at me. I explained that I was doing some research for an exhibition on the Breton onion men and I had met M. Prigent some years before and had been told that he was now at this retirement home.

The woman asked me to wait a moment and she went looking for another woman. The two women came back and I repeated my request. The second woman then explained to me that Jean-Marie Prigent had died half-an-hour before I had arrived. They had not yet managed to contact his family when I had arrived!

* * *

The Prigent family – distantly related to the same Jean-Marie Prigent – are very special to me. Although I tend to think of them as Marie Le Goff's family. They also live in Santec, the area traditionally linked with Wales. I heard a lot of the family history from Marie Le Goff herself. Her mother had worked in a sardine canning factory on Île de Siek, and the hours of work co-incided with the tide. Crossing over to the island on low tide and returning on the next low tide. "During the Great War I worked at home with my parents – they had a large garden. I never went to school, not one day – but I speak Breton, Welsh, a little English, some French – not a lot of French because I never had any school.

"After the war I went to Llanelli to sell onions with my mother and father. After I got married I would go with my husband and he had a cart and pony and we would go to sell onions around the towns and villages – Pontarddulais, Carmarthen, Gower peninsula. Then I started selling onions in the market in Llanelli and my husband would go with the horse and cart. I would sell onions by the pound and he would sell them by the string. The cockle sellers of Pen-clawdd had a stall next to mine and I would eat a whole bag of cockles every day – and steak and chips for lunch. You can grill a steak quickly, you see, and we never had much time.

"I learnt Welsh very easily in those days – *mam, tad, ch'oar, ki, pen* – the two languages are quite similar. We had a house in the centre of Llanelli, near the Post Office. We would come over on a sailing boat before the Second World War, and I would often be seasick. Sometimes if the wind was not right it could take us a week to get to Swansea."

After the death of Marie Le Goff's husband, her daughter Thérèse and her husband, Sebastien Prigent, went with her to Llanelli. Sebastien had started selling in Scotland, which explains why he speaks just a little Welsh but his English has a strong Welsh accent. Thérèse does not speak much Welsh either – an indication, perhaps, of the decline of the language in the great tinplate town in the course of the 20th century.

In Marie Le Goff's family there was a tradition of women going to Wales with their husbands. They were the exception to the general trend. There was a belief that the rough life and lodgings of the Johnnies was not suitable for the women. Anyhow, someone had to stay at home to tend to the vegetables, the cauliflowers, artichokes - and onions. And look after the children. It was the women, very often, who would organise fresh loads of onions to be sent over during the selling season.

Very few women came over before the Great War but their numbers increased from 1921 and in particular after World War II. These are a few sample years of the number of women who came to Britain with their husbands – 1934 (49), 1955 (38), 1966 (49), 1970 (25), 1971 (15). As far as I know, their numbers never exceeded 50. Their work was to wash the clothes, prepare meals, keep the store tidy and stringing. Marie Le Goff was the only woman I know of who would sell onions.

Sebastien and Therese's children in turn came over to Llanelli. But not to work. Guy and Marie-Josie were sent to Saint Mary's Roman Catholic Primary School in Llanelli – they would spend two terms in Llanelli and one in Brittany. "I remember that we used to have a bottle of milk in the middle of the morning and I used to think that was very nice," Marie-Josie once told me.

"The life of the Johnnies was much easier by that time," continued Marie-Josie. "Daddy always had a car – not a bike like in my grandmother's time.

"When it was time for us to go to secondary school my brother and me would stay in Brittany and come over to Llanelli for the half-term holidays. We would fly from Saint Brieuc to Jersey – wait a long time in Jersey, and then get a plane from Jersey to Cardiff and someone would come to meet us in Cardiff."

To this day Marie-Josie speaks English with a delicious mixture of Welsh and French accents. She is a qualified shorthand typist in the English language.

Marie Le Goff died suddenly in 1991 – she was about 90. As it happened I was with a television crew in Roscoff to make a programme for S4C, the Welsh language television channel, and I was expected to interview her for the programme. She died the day before we arrived and the funeral was on a Monday – the day after we arrived in Roscoff. Instead of interviewing her we had to film the funeral – it was the end of an era. I remember the priest saying in the church – "Marie Le Goff was so well-known and so highly regarded in Wales that when they heard of her death the BBC immediately sent a television crew over to her funeral."

Not quite true, but she was well-known in Wales and had been interviewed in Welsh on television when she was selling onions in

Llanelli market and I once interviewed her in Welsh for a radio programme. At her funeral I could only think of how she sang a Welsh folk song for me – *Hen Fenyw Fach Cydweli* – "The Little Old Woman from Cydweli who sold black sweets." That programme was broadcast a few years before she died and the song was broadcast a number of times.

Some years later the Welsh sculptress Ezzelina Jones, who is famous for her portrayals of characters from Welsh working class life, produced one of Marie Le Goff. It showed her as she was in Llanelli market, in a large warm overcoat and a hat on her head. The original work – in brass – was displayed for some months in *La Maison des Johnnies* in Roscoff. Later it was replaced by a copy in clay which can still be seen at the little museum.

It provoked an interesting reaction. For those – like her family – who remembered Marie Le Goff in Llanelli it was a remarkably accurate work. For those who had only known her at home in Santec and coming to Church in her Breton coiff it was a puzzling experience.

Thérèse and Sebastien have kept in touch with many of the friends they made in Wales – some of whom also had stalls in Llanelli market.

* * *

I had called many times in the hope of seeing Claude Deridan. He lived in a house on the east side of the old port of Roscoff – an area of the town known as Pan-al-leur. He was out fishing, or he had been fishing and was very tired and sleeping. I knew that he had had a serious heart operation and gathered that he had a pace-maker. Then one day I saw him sitting on a bench with his back to Porz Glaz with two other Johnnies, one of whom I had got to know very well. In the warm September sun we talked about Wimbledon, Porthmadog and Cricieth.

Deridan began selling onions in Wimbledon in 1920. He was 16, and according to his own testimony he spoke very little French and no English. Up to then he had worked on the farms around Roscoff. His father had been an onion seller in Porthmadog, a town on the coast of Cardigan Bay, and according to Claude, he spoke Welsh fluently.

However, Claude chose to go to Wimbledon and he settled in easily and happily in this suburb of London. Some of his children had accompanied him on the annual migration. He carried on coming to

Wimbledon until the war. Then after the war he began going to Porthmadog. For many years he chartered a boat and sailed directly from Roscoff to Porthmadog with his onions and Johnnies on board. In his final years he had hired a lorry to bring the onions over on the ferry, sailing directly from the new harbour in Roscoff to Plymouth.

He had certainly been a well known character in the town and he had photographs of himself marching with men from the Porthmadog area on Armistice Sunday. He spoke a little Welsh, enough, no doubt to sell his onions

"Sut dach chi?" How are you?

"Da iawn." Very well.

"Dach chi isho nionod?" Do you want onions?

"Dim isho heddiw, digon i gael, dewch tro nesa. Dach chi isho paned o de?" I don't want any today, I've got plenty, call next time. Would you like a cup of tea?

"Dwi isho dim. Cael un tro nesaf." I won't have anything. I'll have one next time.

But he had enough Welsh to be filmed by the BBC with his bicycle selling onions on the Llŷn Peninsula. I am fairly sure that one of his colleagues in Porthmadog, Jean Guivarc'h, spoke a lot more Welsh. But Jean Guivarc'h was a shy man and he managed to avoid my efforts to have a conversation with him.

Claude Deridan's base in Porthmadog was No 7, Pen-cei, but other onion sellers were based at Tremadog, a little further along the road that travelled north from Porthmadog. They were based in the house where T. E. Lawrence – Lawrence of Arabia – was born. They once shared the accommodation with the Welsh artist and sculptor, Jonah Jones. Lawrence, incidentally, had connections with Brittany and spent time there studying the castles. He had stayed in Dinan and Fougères and travelled around on a bicycle. Perhaps he had got some ideas from the Johnnies!

Chapter 4

From Wales to Scotland

"It was not a comfortable life – we went to make money," Jean-Marie Roignant told me. He had spent his final years as a Johnny in Perth in Scotland, in a building known as City Mill. Sometimes he would take his family over. "My daughter was three years of age when she came with me for the first time and in no time at all she could speak English better than any of us.

"We had electricity and gas but not much else. It was not a life for a woman, nor for a family man for that matter. Living in cold and damp conditions. The choice was to leave the family at home or take them with you – neither was ideal."

After he had managed to accumulate some money, he gave up being a Johnny and settled down to farm in an area called Lagad Vran, near the first round-about on the way from Roscoff to Saint-Pol-de-Leon and close to the railway line.

Roignant had started selling onions in Caernarfon, northern Wales in 1924. He was 12 years of age at the time. He remembered that he came on a sailing boat right into Caernafon. The first job was to unload the onions. He would get sent to sell onions in Anglesey – an island facing Caernafon, as he once described it to me. "I remember I was very small – *comme trois pommes* – and I was selling onions in the market in Llangefni," he said. "At the time I could speak speak Welsh – only Welsh – *'Dos adra'r diawl bach … ty'd yma tro nesa'* (go home you little devil … call next time)." He could still remember all the towns and villages he would visit in Anglesey and Caernarfon.

For his first season in Caernarfon he earned 200 francs – and his food and bed, of course. At the time there were 24 Johnnies in the town. "We had a lot of fun in the store. We lived on potage and bacon. We would have a large piece of boiled bacon. Then the stringer who was also the cook would slice it and then put the pieces behind his back and then he would choose a piece for every Johnny. Of course he would cheat so that any Johnny who could not eat fatty meat, would get a piece that was all fat. We had a lot of fun. On Sundays we would spend the time playing dominoes. We had to go to church – the Catholic Church which was about a mile from Caernarfon Castle. The boss, my uncle Louis Roignant, would give us two pence each to put on the collection plate."

The company also had other centres. They had a stringer in Chester, which is just across the border in England, and they also had a base in Bala. From there Johnnies would go out selling onions around Corwen, Betws-y-coed, Rhuthun and as far as Oswestry – another town across the border in England. "We would take the onions from Caernarfon to Chester and Bala in the two vans we had – two old Ford vans with wooden wheels and two gears for going forward and one for going back."

He learnt Welsh playing with children in the streets of Caernarfon, but Shamar as his friends called him, had to work. "I am sure I was no more than 14 years of age when I used to drive one of these vans around Anglesey. I would drop the sellers off in the villages and they would go off to sell around the farms and I would come to pick them up in the evening and take them back to Caernarfon."

He had been very happy in Wales and if he had a free afternoon there was nothing he enjoyed better that going to local sheep-dog trials. "Those were the cleverest dogs I ever saw in my life. I was in Ruthin market day one day when a flock of sheep bolted through the town. In a flash a dog went after them and in no time at all he had rounded them and brought them back to where they were supposed to be.

"I bought one of those dogs and brought it back to Brittany with me. My greatest pleasure when I was in Caernarfon was to watch a dog at work with a flock of sheep or herd of cattle. In the sheep-dog trials, I simply couldn't understand how a dog could work three sheep in that way."

He remembered the occasion when the Dolgarrog dam burst in North Wales. Water swept through the entire village. It was pure chance that all the people happened to be in a meeting in the village hall which was on higher ground than the village – otherwise all the population would have drowned. "We were on our way home from Corwen fair and had stopped in the hotel in Dolgarrog for a drink. I am sure we left the place minutes before the dam burst. We didn't know anything about the disaster until a couple of days later when we saw pictures in a newspaper of dead sheep and cattle in the fields."

Jean-Marie Roignant did not say long in Caernarfon. He never got on with the boss, his uncle Louis Roignant. Although they were related they quarrelled bitterly and in 1927 Jean-Marie went to sell onions in Guernsey and in 1929 he went to Perth in Scotland. By now he was the boss. His heart warmed to the land of the glens and he talked with delight about his visits to Oban, Balachulish, Glencoe and Fort William.

In Perth he had eight in his company – including his wife, his daughter, an uncle (not Louis!) and four sellers. He said that his wife never learnt much English but she could string as well as any man.

He had a brother who was killed in World War II. He was also a Johnny with his base in Stornoway, on the Isle of Lewes. "He was in a party with Charcot and his sailors the night before the Pourquoi Pas sailed to its disaster in the North Sea." Jean-Marie Roignant's brother would have been the last Frenchman, apart from the crew, to have seen Charcot alive.

Jean-Marie Roignant was a small, lively, man and a lively tongue. "A real communist," Jean-Marie Cueff described him to me. He admitted to me that he admired the works of Emile Zola and he was fiercely critical of the way the Government in Paris treated Brittany.

He died about 1994.

* * *

A typical South Wales valleys man is considered to be cheerful, witty, an extrovert with a short fuse but who will simmer down just as quickly. Pierre Guivarc'h, who lived in Dossen, was just that sort of character. He first came to Swansea with his father in 1921. He was nine years old at the time. And it was to Swansea that he came for the next 17 years sailing every year, he claimed, on the *Iris*, a ship which apparently sank with a load of coal near Île de Batz a few years before the war. It was on its way back having delivered a load of onions and a number of Johnnies to Swansea.

"About 60 of us came over in sailing boats, three or four ships coming together," he said.

He obviously had a warm regard for the Welsh although these had been difficult times. There was the 'Buy British' movement of the early Thirties which he said had affected the Johnnies. "Some people wouldn't look at us, but most people accepted that we had a job to do. And they would buy from us." He lit another Gitanes – Pierre was one of the few Johnnies who did not roll his own cigarettes – and coughed with the commitment of an old coal miner. "I could get on with the

Welsh – well, we're all Welsh, all Celts anyway. It was only on one occasion that I ever had any trouble. I was nine years old and having my mid-day soup on the Strand in Swansea when a policeman came up to me. I remember him – he was from Fforest Fach (a village just outside Swansea). He said I was too naughty and cheeky for a nine year old. I may have been cheeky but I was never naughty."

Pierre was in Swansea when the war began and he was among those who were ordered to return immediately. He had a brother in the company who was too young to be called up and he had to stay on to sell the remaining onions. Pierre was taken prisoner of war near Dunkirk and spent the war in a camp in Breslav, Poland. He learnt German very rapidly and soon became fluent in Polish as well. As a result he was made to work as a translator by the Germans.

"The Germans would tell me that they would have Churchill cleaning out the stables in Germany after the war. I would reply that once the war was over Hitler would digging coal in a South Wales colliery. They didn't like that. I don't like the Germans. One reason I can't go selling onion now is that they got my legs. I'll talk to the young ones, but never the old ones."

In spite of the fact that he had never had a day's formal schooling, Pierre was a remarkable linguist. He spoke five languages fluently and evidently at one time he had more than a smattering of Welsh.

One evening we were in a café in Dossen when he got into an argument with a student who was serving behind the bar. Somehow, the student made a comment about speaking "dying languages". Pierre got very excited. "So how many languages do you speak?" asked Pierre. "German," said the student "and French." "So you speak German do you? And how well do you speak German?" "Fluently" replied the student. "Very well then, let's talk to each other in German," responded Pierre, and a torrent of German burst from his lips. When it was obvious to everyone that the old onion man's German was much better than that of the student, he reverted to speaking French. "And the reason why I speak all these languages? I never turned my back on my first language – Breton – and that has been the language I have always spoken here in Dossen and in the warehouse when I was a Johnny."

After the war Pierre resumed his trade. "I went first to Newcastle-on-Tyne, but I never really got on with the Geordies so I went to Aberdeen the following year. When I was in Swansea the Welsh told me they never got on with Scots. Well, I got on very well with them all – Welsh and Scots. But I never trusted the Geordies. When I was in Swansea I used to sell onions to a Professor in the University – his name was Diveres. Later, when I went to Aberdeen I met his son who was a lecturer at the University there." Diveres was in fact the name of a Breton and a distinguished Celtic scholar who had in fact been at Swansea University.

Pierre remained in Aberdeen until he retired from selling onions in 1974.

That night, in the café in Dossen he argued and drank until it was well beyond what the woman I assumed to be the owner considered an appropriate time to close. "Don't take any notice of her, hell, I'm a good customer" was the only response I got to my suggestions that we should leave.

I saw him for the last time in 1991. He looked much older than the youngish looking man I had spent so much time listening to his reminiscences ten years earlier. My lasting memory is of him wobbling off down the road on his bicycle in a cloud of cigarette smoke.

* * *

It is not difficult to appreciate why the Johnnies were so fond of Wales. In the old days, all the Johnnies were Breton speakers and they were comfortable amongst the Welsh people, and most of them appeared to be aware of a similarity in the languages and of some common, historical past. Celine Habasque, a student at Brest University who wrote a dissertation about the Johnnies for her degree said that, bearing in mind the size and population of Wales, a disproportionately high percentage of Johnnies went to Wales. She suggests that this could be explained through some historical and linguistic awareness.

They had something in common with Scotland, too, although, according to Celine the Johnnies did not start going to Scotland until 1902. I don't know whether she was right, because it is certainly contrary to what Joseph Corre, who went Orkney and Shetland, told me. He said that his father had done 48 seasons in Scotland – and assuming that his father never came after 1939 – he must have been coming over in the 19th century, well before 1902. But if, somehow, Celine is correct then the growth in the trade of the Johnnies must have been very rapid.

The "Welsh" Johnnies came from Santec and Dossen. The "Scottish" Johnnies tended to be from the town of Roscoff. They were all aware, and proud, of the town's connections with Scotland. Mary Stuart landed in Roscoff, a plaque shows where she disembarked in 1548, and Bonnie Prince Charlie arrived in the town's little harbour some months after Culloden. The Johnnies – like most of the town's inhabitants – were proud of the Auld Alliance.

Ballerno is a small town outside Edinburgh on the way to Lanark. There, according to Claude Tanguy, live the nicest people in the world. In fact, they are so nice that he named his house, which is in the part of Roscoff known as Kernaguer, Ballerno.

Claude Tanguy, himself one of the most pleasant and helpful of people, began selling onion in 1928 – he was then 13. He was based at Leith, the port of Edinburgh. "I remember 110 Johnnies coming to Leith in 1935/1936," he said. Tanguy was a mine of information and his home an archive of old documents about the lives of the Johnnies. These included contracts with shipping companies and stores, and cuttings from newspapers. When I was collecting material for the exhibition for *La Maison des Johnnies* his assistance and knowledge were invaluable. He was also an expert on Scotch whiskies!

"The Johnnies who went to Scotland were the ones who left first, because they had the furthest to go, and they would have the first crop of onions," he said. "We would return for Christmas and then go back to sell until the end of February. If there were onions to sell and no work in Brittany we might stay in Scotland until the end of April. But traditionally, the end of February was the end of the season.

"There were large families in Roscoff in those days, and everyone who went to sell onions was one mouth less to feed back home. One old Johnny was telling me last week how his little brother had wandered on to an onion boat while they were loading and the boat sailed while he was still on board! He was away from home for six months!"

He had memories of hard masters. "We never worked on Sundays, but we had to get up at a quarter past midnight on Monday morning to string onions as we had done no work on Sunday. Mind you, the bosses were just as hard on themselves. Many times I walked 20 miles with a load of onions on my back or pushing a wheelbarrow full of onions. More than once the police stopped me at night because I had no light on the barrow! But on the whole we were on good terms with the police. They often came to the warehouse for a cup of tea."

He retired from selling onions in 1975 following an operation. Then two years later he returned to Scotland for a holiday. He immediately called on one of his old friends who was still selling onions in Edinburgh and asked if he could have a few strings to sell. Then, with all the time in the world, he called on his old customers. "And I would accept all those cups of tea, glasses of port, or wine or whisky I had refused over the years. When I was selling onions it was always a problem having to refuse all these kind offers. If I accepted a cup of tea in one house, others to whom I had said no, would ask me 'What's the matter with me? Why don't you accept my tea?' And they could get quite cross."

So by going back on holiday, he sold some onions for his friend and could spend all day talking to old friends, visit every one and offend none.

He was, as I said the nicest of men. I remember talking to him on one occasion when he had just given two young Scottish lads free lodging for a week. They were wearing kilts and he had gone to speak to them. The boys hardly had two words of French between them, they had failed to find somewhere to stay and had spent a night sleeping under an upside down boat on Carantec beach. One of the lads recognised him immediately – "You used to sell onions to my mother," he said.

There was a certain humour about his methods. He and his friends had a card which they pushed through the letterboxes of regular customers – "*Onion Johnnie est arrive*". Just like the Beaujolais nouveau!

His favourite relaxation when in Scotland was watching Hibernian Football Club, although he would be out selling onions immediately after the match. His son had been with him selling onions in Scotland and on one occasion his three daughters had been there at the same time working as *au pairs*.

On the wall of his lounge was a painting of a street in Edinburgh with the castle in the background. The work of John Fielder. I saw Claude Tanguy for the last time when I visited him in hospital a little while before he died. It was about 1996.

* * *

Just like Claude Tanguy, "Peta Claude" Corre was another mine of information about the Johnnies. I remember him sitting on a low wall staring out to sea. "Come for a chat, I've got plenty of good material for you indoors." "Indoors" was a first floor flat in Rue Jules Ferry. He leant heavily on his walking stick, but if he moved slowly his speech was lively and colourful. On the door of his apartment was his name, Claude Corre, embroidered over a piece of Scottish tartan. To the people of Glasgow he was "Peta Claude" – and many people in Roscoff knew him by that name. He invited me to sit at the table and he took a box out of the cupboard and handed me a cutting from a Scottish newspaper. There was a picture of him, with a necklace of onions around his neck and behind him on the wall was a picture of Robert Burns.

I noted a few lines from the story: "The strangest most warm-hearted tribute to Robbie Burns comes from a stocky little 'Ingan Johnnie' who believes with all his heart in the Auld Alliance. He boasts that he has sold onions to four generations of one family in Cellardyke in Fyfe. ('After France, Scotland is ma country and Glesca's ma toon')."

The story went on to explain the circumstances in which the photograph was taken. 'Peta Claude' was a guest of honour at the Our's Club Burns night and it was reported that he had sung his own translation into Breton of one of Burns's best known songs, *Ye Banks and Braes*. He showed me another picture of himself, a picture taken on his first visit to Scotland in 1920 when he was only eleven years of age. With him in the picture was his father – also a very short man, with a large cap and a heavy moustache – and a rather tall prosperous looking customer. Another newspaper clipping revealed that Mary Stuart was one of his heroines. After all, had she not sailed from Tantallon Castle, Berwickshire, to Roscoff in 1548 when she was just five years of age?

Also among the papers was a copy of a letter sent by the Johnnies of Roscoff to Lady Clementine Churchill at the time of the death of her husband, Winston Churchill.

"Dear Lady Churchill,
    "In the name and on behalf of all the Roscoff onion merchants I wish to express to you the deep sorrow and grief we feel on the

passing of Sir Winston Churchill. We owe him our gratitude for all he has done for France in the last war and we cannot forget that it is thanks to him that we are free people today and that we are able to come over to your country to bring our products.

"Please accept from us all the sincerest expression of sympathy and may God give you all the strength and courage to bear your great sorrow.

Johnnies de Roscoff."

I never met an onion seller with a greater enthusiasm for the area where he had been selling, than Corre. As well as being a fan of Robert Burns he was a fanatic supporter of Glasgow Celtic Football Club. He claimed that he never missed a home game in all the years he had been coming to Scotland. "I was at Hampden Park, I think it was in 1948, when Scotland played Hungary and Puskas was in Hungary's team that day. What a player – he scored a goal and I'm sure the goalkeeper never saw the ball. I was shouting like hell for Scotland but that Puskas was a genius. Aye I'm a Scotsman, or at least I was a Scotsman when I was in Glasgow. Mind you, some Scots are better than others. Take the people of Greenock, they'd take the sugar out of your tea."

Tea was all very well, but 'Peta Claude' preferred something stronger. "I never sold onions on the morning after a Burns Night – I always had a bad head. Usually I drank Younger's Strong Ale and whisky on special occasions, like on Burns Night and Hogmanay. I loved a drop of Johnny Walker but I couldn't stand the smell that came from their distillery. Once I tried to sell onions outside their gates – I had to go away, the smell was terrible. There should have been a law against it." He put two glasses on the table and filled them to the brim with red wine. "First today," he said, raising his glass, "that's what they used to say in Scotland. First today, never the last, always the first! Iec'hed mad!"

He asked me where I was staying. I replied that I was staying in Kerlouan. "Ah, Kerlouan," he said. "That's the place for garlic, the best garlic in the world is grown in Kerlouan." 'Peta Claude' was prone to exaggeration. "I used to sell three tons of garlic every year between the Glen Eagles and the Central Hotel in Glasgow. Both hotels had French chefs and I was always welcome in both – and breakfast if I wanted it. I used to sell a lot of onions to these hotels as well as the garlic. I remember that I would sell four bags (56 lbs each) every week to the Central Hotel, Glasgow, on top of what I would sell to the Glen Eagles and the Grand Hotel, Saint Andrews."

Many years after that conversation – and many years after 'Peta Claude' had died – my wife and I got into conversation with a Scottish couple. It was a Sunday morning and we were having an aperitif at the Chez Janie, Roscoff, before lunch. The man suddenly said that he had just visited this delightful little museum about the Johnny Onion men. It was the little museum I had helped to establish a couple of years earlier. For some reason he misinterpreted my smile and got excited and started lecturing me about these Breton Onion Men, and this museum had pictures of his old friend ... The old friend, it turned out, was 'Peta Claude' and the Scotsman had himself been a chef in one of Glasgow's smart hotels. He had been one of 'Peta Claude's regular customers. So there I was hearing of the popularity of 'Peta Claude' from an old friend. A few days later I took them around the museum myself, just in case they had not believed me.

When he was eleven years old, 'Peta Claude' had tried to get some extra work, so that he could pay to go to night school. "I managed to get two months of night school for three years – that's all the school I ever had. But I learnt the important things – how to count money, write a bit and read. But I spent more time learning from experience."

When he was fifteen, he suffered what I assumed to be some kind of minor brain haemorrhage, and had to go to hospital for treatment. After he had been released he had to go back for a weekly check-up. "I remember the doctor telling my father during one of these visits that no lad of my age and state of health should be living in such conditions. But in no time at all I was out selling onions again – but not too near the hospital in case one of the doctors should see me."

His views on the customers were interesting. "The Italians were good buyers and the French Chefs – although the red onion of Roscoff is not their favourite, they prefer the yellow onions grown around Saint-Brieuc, Langueux and Yffiniac. But those yellow onions, they don't keep so well, you see. I remember the Gorbals in Glasgow full of Jews – they were hard bargainers, but I could do business with them. I didn't get on so well with the Pakistanis who came later – always on the lookout for the cheapest stuff."

Like all the onion sellers, the war interrupted his trade. But he was back in 1947. "We were selling wholesale that first year, the English

Government wouldn't let us sell in our traditional way. We took 55 tons to Southampton. After that we were allowed to sell again in the old way, thanks to François Mazeas. He was a very clever man, and very determined. It was a long and hard fight before everything was settled but in the end we were given assurances that we could continue our old trade in our traditional way."

I visited him regularly for weeks, always bringing a bottle of red wine – he talked better if he had wine. Or so he said.

All the Johnnies I ever met lived in pleasant, smart houses – all, except 'Peta Claude'. His home was a tiny, modest flat in a somewhat grim building.

I remember the last time I saw him. We walked from his flat to the little wall where he would sit and look out to sea. An elegant French woman came over and gave him a gentle nagging about his smoking. As usual, and like all Johnnies, 'Peta Claude' had the remnant of a hand rolled cigarette between his lips. "Hell, it's my health and I'll do as I like with it," he said. But he said it with no rancour and no trace of a suggestion that she should mind her own business. We talked briefly then, curiously, she asked who I was. I said that I was researching the history of the onion men of Roscoff. She had been retired for some years in Roscoff, without having even heard of the Johnnies. I told her of the popularity of these men of Roscoff who migrated annually to Britain to sell their onions. Slowly, she began to see the scruffy little man in a different light. This was no longer the little man who smoked too much and drank too much. Here was a multi-lingual little man, with a colourful history who translated Robert Burns into Breton. "Robert ... who?" she asked.

I said goodbye and left 'Peta Claude' in full flow lecturing the lady about the greatest poet in the history of the world. 'Peta Claude' was prone to a little exaggeration. The next time I called he was dead.

* * *

I met Joseph Corre just once. At the time I had not met "Peta Claude" Corre, and I never knew whether they were related. It sounds incredible, but here was a wiry little onion seller who went to Orkney and Shetland. He worked his small farm on the outskirts of Roscoff, an area known as Pen-al-lan overlooking the wide estuary leading up to Morlaix. His farm was on the right on the way to one of Roscoff's little tourist attractions, the *Jardin Exotique*, near the Roscoff Ferryport.

When Joseph Corre went to the islands for the first time with his father in 1925 he was only 13 years of age. He was, nevertheless, a seasoned onion seller having already spent two years apprenticeship selling in Aberdeen. Then, in 1925, his father who, according to Joseph, did a total of 48 seasons selling onions on the islands, decided it was time for his son to get to know his future customers on the distant, northerly islands.

With seven or eight hampers – each one containing 260 kilos of onions already strung, he went with his father to Kirkwall and Stormness on Pomona, the largest of the Orkney islands. The pattern was to spend six weeks selling there, return to Aberdeen, fill up the hampers and then off to Lerwick, the largest of the Shetland islands. He would spend a month there, return to Aberdeen and then back again to Orkney.

"My onions were kept in the same stores as the Johnnies who were based in Aberdeen," he said. "I had my own stringer there. I would call on my customers twice every season and when I walked down the streets with my onions people ran out of their houses and after me to buy the onions. I had no competition, so I could charge more for my onions.

"I remember in that warehouse in Aberdeen there were 25 Johnnies in 1935. Between us we had 400 tons of onions – but I was the only one who went out to the islands.

"I would start out from Roscoff in July and arrive home sometime around Christmas, although I remember more than once celebrating Hogmanay on the islands."

For breakfast, when on the islands, he would have porridge, bacon and eggs; beef and potatoes – or as he said "beef 'n' tatees" – for lunch, a biscuit and a cup of tea – or copotee - around 4.30pm and something similar before going to bed.

He could boast that he had sold onions in John O'Groats and he remembered crossing from Thurso to Stromness in a gale. Another of his memories was reading a newspaper at midnight in July – without any light.

When World War II began his father stayed on for a while to sell what remained of the onions while Joseph went home to fight. He spent five years as a prisoner of war near Hamburg. After the war, he never returned to the islands but settled down to farm his small holding at Pen-al-lan growing onions, carrots and tomatoes. I noticed the little black onion seeds drying in the sun in front of the house but he said that his son did most of the work.

Like many of the Johnnies he reminded me of the people to whom he had sold his onions – tough, little crofters eking out a hard living fishing a tempestuous sea and scraping the thin soil of an equally rough hinterland. He spoke English rapidly, with a strong accent, pronouncing Scotland as Sgotland. Like other onion sellers, he still enjoyed some of the habits he had picked up in Scotland – playing darts and rings and always a "copotee" around 4.30 in the afternoon.

* * *

Jean Berthou was born in 1897, and when I met him for the first and only time he had just celebrated his 81st birthday. He was a sprightly old man, steady on his feet and his memory crystal clear. There were workmen renovating an old cottage at the end of his garden, a cottage with massive walls of huge, rough stones fitted together with splendid craftsmanship. He did all the work in his large garden himself apart from a little help from a nephew who with a horse drawn plough would turn the soil over for him at the beginning of the season.

Berthou had started selling onions in Scotland in 1912 when he was fifteen. Two years later he was on his way to Aberdeen when the Great War started. The war broke in August, and the Johnnies had left Roscoff the day after the Pardon of Sainte Barba – the third Monday of July. Some had even left earlier.

In those days there was no way of contacting a ship once it had sailed. Jean Berthou sailed to Aberdeen on *Les Jumelles* – two other ships sailed with them, *La Roscovite* and *L'Hermann*, all carrying onions to Aberdeen. The first news that Jean Berthou and his colleagues had of the war was when the French consul met them on the quay and ordered everyone within the enlisting age to return home immediately. There were furious arguments. Eventually the Bretons were given three days to try to sell their onions. After that they went by rail to London and made the shortest ferry crossing to France. Not everyone had to leave within that time. Those who were too young or too old to go to war were allowed to stay a little longer to try and dispose of the onions as best they could. Jean Berthou was among those who were too young to fight. Following the swift departure of

71

all men of fighting age, including sailors on the boats as well the Johnnies, there was another problem. The captains of the sailing boats had very few sailors left to help take the boats back to Roscoff.

Captain Koadou of *La Roscovite* was in the worst predicament of all. Beside himself he had a cabin boy, one sailor and an officer to get his boat back to Roscoff. Koadou was determined not to be blockaded in Aberdeen for the rest of the war – even if everyone, in Britain at least, insisted it would "all be over by Christmas". Eventually, he found four men prepared to sail with him back to Roscoff – Jean-Françoise Corre, aged 16, from Roscoff, Claude Creignou, a 65 year old stringer known as *"Glaoda ar sarjant"* because he had been a sergeant in the Franco-Prussian War in 1870, and Jean Berthou from Cleder, at the time aged 17. The ship was loaded with coal in Kircaldy before they set off on the long and hazardous journey home. It took them nearly a month – not because of the volunteer crew's lack of experience, but because there was no wind. "We were even trying to go looking for wind, but had no luck," said Berthou. It has been claimed that the captain was also trying to avoid being seen by German warships. But Berthou did not believe that story. He insisted that the only difficulty had been the unusual calm. When *La Roscovite* sailed into Roscoff one morning in the beginning of September 1914 we can only wonder which was the greater, the relief of those on board or the unexpected pleasure of their families.

Within months Jean Berthou was old enough to become a soldier and he fought through to the end of the war. In 1924 he returned to Scotland to renew his former trade. He showed me a picture of himself selling onions with the *vaz* over his shoulder, it had been taken about 1933. But by then the bicycle was already a more popular and effective tool for carrying strings of onions. "I had my regular customers. They would never buy onions from another Johnny," he said. He talked about his route – Berwick-on-Tweed, Dunbar, Peebles, Galashiels, Selkirk, Melrose, Kelso – "a lovely country". With his bicycle he would visit each one of those towns once every three weeks. Normally he would be back in Brittany before Christmas. He talked about the route home at the end of the season. "We usually went by train to Folkestone, sail from there to Boulogne and home by train through Paris. It was a very quick route. Sometimes we would sail from Southampton to Cherbourg and on one or two occasions I remember sailing directly to Morlaix."

Like so many "ingan Johnnies" he had a soft spot in his heart for Scotland. "Now, take Berwick. That was a place to sell onions. All the hotels had French chefs – it was a great place to do business." Although he had stopped selling onions many years before that he had returned to Scotland for a holiday in 1976. When I spoke to him in 1978 he was crossing regularly for his holidays, but usually in Cornwall.

He was clearly sad when I said that I had to leave and he hurried to get his bottle of whisky and two glasses. The furniture in his house would have graced a museum. In the kitchen there was a large table with a bench which went completely around it. It was not difficult to imagine little children climbing on to the bench and with shiny bottoms sliding round to the far side. The table and bench had been made to fit that particular room. Suspended from the ceiling was a wooden disc with eight holes which held eight forks and eight wooden spoons. "We were seven brothers and one sister," he explained. He also had an old butter churn, the type with a hole in the top in which a stick was placed. I had never seen one like it except in a museum. In addition to his antique furniture and various gadgets from bygone days he had a fine collection of old books in Breton and French, as well as a number of school photographs from around 1900 with all the children in traditional costume. It was a rare treat to meet a man who took such delight in things from his past. His heritage was in his home.

Chapter 5

Two Johnnies in Cardiff

"No home, no comforts, walking through wind and rain in all weather. Getting soaked, and having to remain in those clothes from morning to night. Eating cold onions and the occasional crust of dry bread. And Sunday, it's the saddest day of all for us when we're in Wales. No cathedral like the one in Saint-Pol. No praying or singing Breton and Latin ... And no dressing up for Sunday ... Many people in Wales think that we're tramps." (An onion-seller speaking to Welsh writer Ambrose Bebb in the 1930s).

Bute Street, Cardiff, has some notoriety and not a little romance. To people from outside Cardiff it conjures visions of "women of the night", a place where policemen walked in twos and threes. Today, the original houses have all been destroyed and other houses built to replace them. In fact many of the houses in this long street that links the centre of Cardiff with Cardiff's Docks look as if they, too, are fit to be demolished. Houses in Britain built to replace slums in the years after World War II also became slums themselves.

When Jean-Marie Cueff and Olivier Bertevas spent their last winter in Bute Street in 1977 – 1978 a few of the original buildings at the end nearest to the centre of Cardiff were still standing. Number 253 was among them, a condemned shop. This was their base, from here they wheeled their bicycles under a load of onions around the streets of Cardiff – or, rather eccentrically, Cueff would hire a taxi to go further a-field, particularly Bryn-mawr on the border of the Gwent Valleys and Breconshire. This would have been at least an hour and a half's drive at the end of the 1970s.

In what would have been the shop area, sacks of onions were stacked from the floor to the ceiling. One evening I nearly tripped over a bucket that was full of water. "Does the roof leak?" I asked. "No, but I do," said Cueff. "It's a long way to go for a piss in the middle of the night. From upstairs down to the cellar and out the back." There was no indoor toilet here. In a smaller room in the back a stew of meat, onions and potatoes simmered on a camping stove. It was in this same room that the two men would string their onions. Against the wall there was a mini hayrick of reeds, the water from them seeping across the floor, and balls of raffia for stringing. A few days earlier the two men had been to a farm a little way outside Cardiff where they had been cutting the reeds. "We have to cut the rushes, pay for them and hire a lorry to fetch them," said Jean-Marie. "We have to pay our way at all times." Olivier added: "It cost us £300 to hire a lorry to bring the onions over."

An old shop was ideal because of the large front room where they could keep the sacks of onions, stacked from floor to ceiling. The previous year they had a house in Adamsdown in Cardiff. A house was not ideal because the sacks of onions had to be stored in a number of small rooms.

They would string the onions very quickly and the strings of onions increased very rapidly. It was also remarkable how swiftly, in the course of a few weeks, the sacks of onions in the front room would diminish. They spoke Breton to each other. I always felt that they were happier speaking English than French. "I speak only Breton to my children," said Jean-Marie. "But most of the time they reply in French. I always speak Breton to my wife, it is much easier to quarrel in Breton. But I write to her in French, although I can write Breton." Both knew a few phrases of Welsh although neither had ever worked in Welsh-speaking Wales. Olivier, in particular, was aware of the development of Welsh medium primary schools and could name a number of towns in the valleys where there was a Welsh medium school.

Jean-Marie – I soon learnt that the local people called him Jimmy – preferred to talk about how hard the life of a Johnny was. They would get up at five in the morning, have breakfast of bacon and eggs, or a boiled egg, and would be out in the streets with their bikes by eight. By about four they would be back in the shop stringing onions and would carry on until 5.30pm. Then they would shuffle off up the road to the Custom House, then a popular pub near the city centre end of Bute Street. Shuffle was the word, back at the shop Olivier always wore his sabots (clogs), with a pair of slippers inside the sabots. It was always two pints, but if they had a journalist like myself with them, who would buy them a few more beers they were quite happy to stay longer.

The Custom House, like many working class pubs in Cardiff in those days served only a traditional dark mild beer, brewed by Brains - the city's oldest and by then, only, brewery. Olivier, since he had always worked in Cardiff, always drank this beer. Jean-Marie, whose original base had been Brynmawr, had only settled in Cardiff after the death of Bertevas's brother-in-law Vincent Cabioch and never got to like this particular beer. He drank a keg beer, also brewed by Brains – and generally complained about its taste. Jean-Marie Cueff had got used to a beer brewed by a company known as Rhymney and Crosswells in Gwent. The company had long disappeared – taken over – by 1979. He praised the brew even though he claimed that he had never drank anything alcoholic until he was 30!

Like most Johnnies they were very critical of French and German beers, and enthused about the beers of the places that had become their second home.

Once Jean-Marie and Olivier got back to the shop they carried on stringing, then eat their supper, the meat and onion stew, which often lasted from Monday to Thursday and was heated up every evening on the camping stove. Then at 8.30pm the two would go out again for two pints, this time at the Glendower, another rather grubby pub nearby. Like the Custom House it has long been pulled down in the course of Cardiff's re-development. "I drink too much, especially when I am at home in Brittany," said Jean-Marie. "I will drink wine all day if I'm left alone when I am at home. It's good for me to come to Cardiff – to drink less." They would usually drink two pints at 12.30pm as well as their four pints each in the evenings – which might seem rather a lot of beer to consume in one day.

Olivier sold in the traditional way. With onions on his bicycle he walked through the streets of Cardiff and people would come running after him. By the 1970s neither ever knocked on doors. "I sold 70 strings in 15 minutes on a street corner the other day," said Cueff. In 1977, 70 strings at a £1 a string in a quarter of an hour would have been good selling. But he was probably exaggerating as they could only carry 40 strings on the bike. It was never necessary to haggle over the price. "I remember the time we sold onions for one and sixpence a string and getting haggled down to nine pence," said Jean-Marie.

The crops would vary from year to year. A dry summer in Roscoff and the onions would be small, and if the stems – or tails - had withered too much they were difficult to string. In 1977 the onions were excellent – those of 1976 were poor.

Olivier Bertevas came to Cardiff for the first time in 1925. It was on a sailing boat, coming directly from Roscoff to Cardiff. The boat sailed almost to the door of the customs house – not the pub – along the West

Bute Dock. This dock was filled in and dried many years ago and it was in a warehouse in Collingdon Road – a street running parallel to Bute Street – that they kept their onions, and indeed lived.

Sometimes ten or twelve slept on the hard sacks full of onions in the warehouse which was right on the edge of the dock. The ship would then load up with coal and return to Roscoff. With a fair wind the ships would make the crossing in 26 hours, but if the weather was unfavourable the journey could take five days. Jean-Marie Cueff remembered that he had once crossed in a sailing boat that had taken nine days due to a dead calm and thick fog. These were small ships carrying about 100 tons of onions. He remembered *L'Herman* and *L'Oceanie* sailing from Roscoff to Cardiff before returning with a load of Welsh coal. "They would sail up the West Bute Dock and we would unload the onions from the boat straight onto the train to take them to Brymawr." Sometimes they would sail in a ship owned by a man called Kervizec from Perros Guirec but usually they sailed directly from Roscoff to Cardiff.

Cueff had come over for the first time in 1919 when he was nine years old. "I have slept on rougher floors than this hundreds of times," he once told, looking at the black linoleum floor of the Custom House. There was no problem in getting permission to be absent from school – not that he ever had much school. To learn English was considered to be sufficient education. He knew a man from Plougoulm, Jean-Marie Marrec, who came over with his father and would attend one of the schools near the Cardiff Docks. "He never came over after his father retired, but he can still speak English better than either of us."

Cueff's wages for that first season were 30 francs and a pair of boots. And, his food and lodging, such as it was. The 30 francs were a year's rent for his unmarried mother. "I didn't have a word of English and only a little French. My mother could speak nothing but Breton. She would take in washing – and wash the clothes in the river. I have no idea who my father was – for all I know I had two or three of them."

He always praised the welcome he had received in Wales. The only bitter experiences he could recall was an occasion when some men in the industrial valleys had tried to steal his onions. It was 1926, the year of the Great Strike, and he was just 15 years of age at the time. "Yes, those were bad days. People would steal the clothes off your back if you were not careful." As he was carrying the onions around on the stick – *ar vaz* – those men were literally trying to steal the onions off his back, if not his clothes. Yet he was philosophical about his experiences. "I must admit there has always been more good around than evil, even in those dark days." Brynmawr had been Jean-Marie Cueff's base from 1919 until he went into partnership with Olivier Bertevas in 1972.

Bertevas was following in his father and grandfather's footsteps. Both had been Johnnies before him. Cardiff had been his base from the first time he came over at the age of 14 and he had always sold his onions around the city. "Sometimes I would take my bike with its load of onions on a train up the valleys, but not often," he said. Cueff, however, would often return to his old haunts in Brynmawr and the valley towns and villages. "I hire a car and in a day I can sell onions in Bargoed, Ystrad Mynach and Caerphilly," he told me. "It costs me £3 an hour and the petrol, but it's worth it."

Both had set up in business on their own in the 1930s. "We had to pay for the onions before we started our journey," said Bertevas. "You got no credit from the farmers in those days." For Cueff it was continuous hard work. He worked hard on the farms during the spring and summer to raise the capital needed to buy onions for the autumn and winter. Living as frugally as possible to scrape enough capital to buy the onions, with most of the profits going to buy next year's onions. "I would not buy a steak today so that I could buy more onions tomorrow."

They were taken prisoners in 1940, near the French and Belgium border, and spent the next five years in German prisoner of war camps. Cueff had been sent to Austria where he spent the war working on a farm. It was obvious that his time there had been quite good – he even praised it. There was plenty of food and he even made his own wine. As he once told me that he had never tasted a drop of alcohol until he was thirty, this must have been the time when he started. "I would take a drop before breakfast and I was 29 pounds heavier at the end of the war than I was when it began," he said. As well as that there was a woman who wanted him to stay in Austria and marry her. He refused as he already had a wife in Brittany.

Bertevas's wartime experiences were less agreeable. He was forced to work in a factory making springs and parts for guns. "The heat was terrible – unbearable. We wore nothing but shorts." Later he was transferred to work on a farm and he had been much happier. There was no point in trying to escape, he said. Some of his fellow prisoners had tried but they had all been caught eventually. Anyway, what was the point? The Germans were in Brittany, too. He would face a long period in hiding in his own country in a great deal of danger. He was 29 when the war started, perhaps a little old for such heroics. By the time he was released he was 34, and he married soon afterwards.

Bertevas started selling onions again in Cardiff in 1951, in partnership with a friend. That man died in Saint David's Hospital, Cardiff, two years later, in 1953. He had been suffering from high blood pressure. His wife had come over with Bertevas's wife just before he died. "His wife was anxious to take his body back to buried in Brittany, but it could not be arranged and he had to be buried in Cardiff," said Bertevas. "I had two tons of unsold onions and I sold a ton to a Johnny in Maesteg and the rest to another Cardiff Johnny." From 1954 to 1973 his partner had been his brother-in-law, Vincent Cabioch. Cabioch was killed in January 1973 when he was coming off a Brittany Ferries boat in Roscoff. Until they both retired in 1978 his partner had been Jean-Marie Cueff.

One evening in the Custom House, Cueff began to talk about the songs they sang in the stores when he was part of a large company. I asked him if he knew the story of Ker Ys, about the drowning of a coastal city in Brittany, possibly near Douarnenez. Not only did he know the story but he started singing bits from the ballad:

> *Bezet milliget ar verc'h wenn*
> *A zialc'houezaz, houde koen,*
> *Gore puns Ker Is, mor tremen!*

('A curse on the girl who opened, after the feast, the floodgates of Ker Ys, the sea's barrier.') I asked whether it was the one from the *Barzaz Breiz*, but he did not know. His eyes lit up, and the tiredness of a day selling onions and hours of stringing melted away for a moment. He started reciting the ballad, forgot the words, then he would remember another couplet. "They're all drowned down here," he said, putting his hand on his heart. "But they do come to the surface now and again. They are a part of me." His mother used to sing them to him when he was a child. "And while stringing onions in the days when we were large companies we would sing the old Breton songs of our homeland." Then he started singing again, this time a snippet from a

Breton ballad about the sinking of the Titanic:

Ar Teitanig a zo brazad
Lez betek breman
A-vanke n'en tra varnizi
Plas da'r choari a da'r bourmen.

("The Titanic is a larger vessel than any now, in no way can it be thought deficient, a place for dance and play.")

"I don't care for the new songs which blare out of these transistor radios," he said. He then began telling me about the sinking of the *Hilda*, although his knowledge of the disaster and when it happened was very vague. But it was enough to set me on the trail of the greatest disaster in the history of the Johnnies.

One evening Bertevas told how he had met a "Protestant Priest" in Rhiwbina, one of the suburbs of Cardiff. They had met before and the "Priest" had told him to call. "I did not call," said Bertevas, "I never knock on doors these days. But I was happy to see him and we talked for a while." Bertevas might not knock on doors but he did go into restaurants and shops. On the same day he had called in a wine shop in North Road, Cardiff, sold a number of strings to the proprietor, who had then opened a bottle of wine and they had a few glasses before moving on.

It was October 4, 1977, and although Cueff had had a hard day – the selling outside Cardiff market has been slow – the season was going well. The day before he had arranged for the transfer of £1,700 from the bank in Cardiff to his bank in Saint-Pol-de-Leon. Bertevas mentioned two men from Cardiff, Butt and Morson, who helped the Johnnies in Cardiff – organizing banking facilities and the exchange of money. But he was not sure whether they were being treated fairly by them. Anyhow, very soon, many of the Johnnies had learnt how make such arrangements for themselves. The rent on the shop, £4 a week, was paid in advance until the end of the season, and all other sundry expenses were also paid. Also the £6 per ton of import duty had to paid in advance. Cueff told me that he had transferred another £5,000 to his bank a month later. Very soon after that they returned to Roscoff for another load of onions, 14 tons, for which they paid around £1,300 and £400 for the lorry to bring the onions over. On this occasion they had gone round the farms to buy the onions directly, and saved having

Claude Deridan (with the beret in the centre of the picture) marching with ex-servicemen in Porthmadog on Armistices Sunday.

Deridan and one of his company riding their loaded bicycles in Porthmadog. They did not usually ride the bikes when they were loaded in this way – except for the benefit of newspaper photographers!

Guillaume Le Duff (on the left), Olivier Bertevas (centre) and Vincent Cabioch enjoying Brains Dark in the Custom House in Cardiff.

A company in the North of England.

François Keriven selling onions in the snow in Leeds.

Francois Keriven (left) with one of his colleagues and their van in Darlington.

Today, the Johnnies often sell onions to shops and restaurants as well as from door-to-door. A few strings of Breton onions can be very attractive in a green-grocers shop.

A sailing boat with onions and Johnnies arriving in Poole in the period between the two wars.

Paul Caroff selling onions in Poole.

Jean-Marie Prigent, who sold onions in Bristol, at his home near Saint-Pol-de-Leon.

The great disaster – the sinking of the Hilda *in 1905 when 74 Johnnies lost their lives. The* Hilda *before she sank.*

The Hilda *on the rocks near Saint-Malo.*

Boats looking for bodies after the Hilda *disaster.*

Artist's impression of the disaster.

There were only six survivors of the disaster, five were Johnnies – Jean-Louis Mouster, Olivier Caroff, Paul Penn, Jean-Louis Rozec, Tanguy Laot – and one sailor, Able-seaman James Grinter.

The memorial in Roscoff to those who had lost their lives.

François Mazeas (centre) with customers in Bradford. Mazeas saved the Johnnies after the Second World War. The British Government passed a law prohibiting any company – or individual – from importing and retailing fruit and vegetables into Britain. This was done to artificially raise the prices of imported products into Britain so that British producers would have an advantage over foreign producers. Thanks to the perseverance and determination of Mazeas the Johnnies – alone – were exempt from this law.

Certificate of Registration (Aliens Act 1920) of Jean-Marie Argouarc'h – popularly known as 'Jimmy Bach' (Little Jimmy) in Newcastle Emlyn.

Membership card of the 'Association des Johnnies' which became obligatory after the Second World War.

"Looks like we're through then!" Gren Jones's cartoon in the South Wales Echo *of December 12, 1990, when the news came that diggers on both sides of the Channel Tunnel had met. Johnny Onions is the stereotype 'Frenchman' for the average Briton to this day.*

89

They were simply selling their onions everywhere in the 1920s and 1930s! Note the Johnny in the picture. Piccallili Cottage by the famous illustrator of folk and fairy tales, Arthur Rackman.

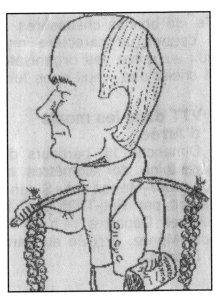

A cartoon of the author by Alan Guivarch in Ouest France, *May 15, 1994.*

The author as a Johnny Onion man publicising an exhibition of the Onion Men and their trade outside Cardigan Museum , Western Mail, *September 26, 1998.*

A map in the Roscoff publicity brochure. Note the prominence given to the Johnnies.

Even little children in Wales know of the Johnnies! Book Day in Wales in 2002 with children in a Welsh school dressed as 'Frenchmen'! With Breton onions – naturally!

Swapping memories on the old quay in Roscoff. From the left: Claude Tanguy (Leith, Scotland), Olivier Creignou (Aberdeen), Olivier Olivier (Haverfordwest), Jean-Marie Roignant (Caernarfon, Guernsey and Perth), Madeleine Le Guerch (former agent) and Sebastien Prigent (Llanelli). The author in the background.

Books on the Johnnies. Launching a Breton language book Paotred an Ognon *(The Onion Boys) with Père Medar signing copies of his book.*

Johnnies du Pays de Roscoff,
a Skol Vreizh publication for schools.

Michel Olivier looking at a previous book by the author, Goodbye Johnny Onions, *in 1989.*

Official launch of an exhibition of the Johnnies and their trade in Pontypridd Museum in 1994. The Roscoff deputation from the left: Josette Gillon, René Bothuan, Patricia Chapalain (deputy mayor and daughter of a former Johnny), Madeleine Le Guerch and Le Telegramme correspondent, Remy Sanquer. The author in the background.

At La Maison des Johnnies *in Roscoff, Sebastien Prigent, Marie-Josie and Thérèse with the picture of the old lady Marie le Goff in the background.*

The author preparing the Johnnies exhibition in Pontypridd museum in 1994.

Section of the exhibition.

A procession of Johnnies to the official opening of La Maison des Johnnies *in Roscoff in 1995. François Keriven (nearest the camera with the onions on the stick); André Quémenér (next to him with the bike). Behind them is Jean Le Roux (with the beret), who until recently went to Highbury, London, and next to him, in the cap, is Guillaume Seité who was going to Bristol while well over 80 years of age. Watching the procession in the background is the Mayor of Taff-Ely Borough Council at the time and now member of the Welsh Assembly, Janet Davies.*

The old port of Roscoff as it is today, full of fishing boats and small sailing craft. The Chapel of Sainte Barbe can be seen in the distance in the centre of the picture.

Today – and the future – Brittany Ferries *carrying vegetables to Britain and tourists to Brittany through Roscoff's deep water port.*

to pay commission to an agent. There had been a first class crop of onions and the farmers did not know what to do with them. Even things like sacks cost money, so they were careful to save them. "They've cost me 20p each and I've got nearly 500 of them."

Cueff liked to pretend to be the tough and cynical one. But Bertevas was the really hard one and Cueff knew it. Cueff would admit that he would drop the price from £1, down as much as to 80p, to sell his last few strings. Bertevas would never drop his price, he was a stubborn man. Some evenings he would stay under a flyover and sell onions to people driving home from work. At least it was dry, but usually very cold. "Olivier is one of the *tud kaled* (hard folk), a real Breton, a real Leonard," said Cueff. They had quarrelled and Cueff was annoyed that Bertevas had been calling him Charlie Chaplin and Cueff had threatened to punch him. "If you can't call a man by his real name, you are not showing him any respect." But Cueff was obviously uncomfortable about the fact that they had quarrelled. He praised Olivier for his diligence and ability to get up in the morning. "I would be happy to stay in bed for a while every morning, if I were left alone. If I were at home with my wife I would not get up until 9," he said.

"My alarm clock has broken and I can't see the time on my watch in the dark, but Olivier is sure to be awake and to get up at 5.30."

On another occasion I was there when they quarrelled because Jean-Marie had hired a car to get some reeds for stringing, but the land was flooded and he had paid a farmer for straw. Olivier was furious that he had paid money for straw. Cueff replied that if he wanted reeds he would have to go and cut them himself on the top of a mountain. Everywhere else was under water.

Shortly before they returned to Roscoff at the beginning of November I remember calling at the shop in Bute Street and I could see no light. I was about to turn back and walk to the Custom House when, for some reason, I looked through the hole in the door where there once had been a lock and could just see a flicker of light in the back room where they did their stringing. I knocked on the door and Bertevas appeared from the gloom, unbarred the door and asked me to come in. He had been trying to get his Wellingtons off, so I helped. And he slipped his feet into the wooden clogs. He complained about having to wear these rubber boots, but at least it was better than walking with his feet wet. He had bought new boots but they had been ruined by the rain. He complained about turning back the clocks.

It was now dark before 5 pm. The only light was a candle flickering in an old wine bottle. I asked why they did not have electric light. Olivier explained that a man from the electricity board had called and discovered the building had no electricity meter. Olivier said he knew nothing about these things. Anyhow their electricity supply was swiftly cut off. The man from the electricity said that he would be back to install a meter and switch the electricity back on in two days – they arranged a time for him to call, 10am. The day the man from the electricity was supposed to have called was that morning. But when I called that same evening there was still no electricity. Olivier explained that he had waited until 10.05am and the man still had not arrived. "I had onions to sell," said Olivier, "I couldn't wait all day for him." So Olivier locked up and left. When they got back that evening a note had been pushed through the door. It was from the electricity man and it said that he had called at 10.15am and there was no one in the shop. So they were still without electricity. He did not appear to mind very much. They had a fire, lumps of coal exchanged for onions! They cooked on a camping stove and they had their candles. And, anyhow, they were about to return to Brittany for more onions. "We will sort it out when we come back," said Olivier.

I never asked, but the next time I went to see them the shop was lit up like a Christmas tree. Many years later, Celine Habasque, a student from Guisseny who made a study of the Johnnies for her degree at the University of Brest told me that it was common practice for the Johnnies to connect their warehouses – illegally – to the electricity or gas and the public water supply. Very often they would have been and gone before the authorities caught up with them. I wonder whether Cueff and Bertevas had gone back home, stayed there for a week and then come back and re-connected themselves to the electricity.

They never went to Church on Sundays when in Cardiff. Cueff thought that the people in the congregation would not like to have two men smelling of onions and garlic amongst them. It was different when they were at home in Brittany with their wives to keep an eye on them. The only day they went to church was All Saints Day, and then they would spend the rest of the day drinking in one of the pubs. They never worked on that day. "It is not the best way to remember your ancestors," said Cueff. "When we're at home our wives make sure that we go to church, although we always go to the café for a drop of wine." It was obvious that he hoped that his son would be remembering him on All Saints Day.

Bertevas said that Cueff had once made a pilgrimage to Lourdes. "I would like to go myself, but only for a weekend. Jean-Marie went for a week," he said. Cueff remembered hearing someone singing in Breton, the ballad *Itroun Varia Rumengol*. I remembered Anatole Le Braz describing something similar in his book *Au Pays des Pardons* when he was going by train to the Pardon at Rumengol.

Olivier said that he had once been to the Pardon at Rumengol – the Pardon of the Singers – where the singers of ballads would come to worship and sing their songs. He regretted that the Sant-Pol pardon was no longer observed. "We had a new priest and he had no interest in the custom. I remember how we would go from house to house collecting wood for the bonfire. We had a lot of fun in those days."

Life for an onion seller in a foreign land was not without its worries. One Sunday morning I joined them for a drink at the Glendower. All around us there were people playing cards or dominoes for money.

"A man knocked on our door a few nights ago and said he had come for a game," said Olivier. "I told him that he was welcome to a game as long as he was prepared to play for onions. I think some men had been running a card school in the shop before we arrived. We never play with anyone. In Brittany it is different. I will enjoy a game in a café – dominoes usually.

"If I win, you buy me a drink; if you win, I buy you a drink. In Cardiff I have seen people betting, a pound or more a go, a pound becomes a five pounds and ten pounds and some poor creature goes home without his pay packet."

They had never got involved – or been tempted to get involved – with women in Cardiff. "Anyhow, we smelt of onions and garlic. What woman would ever look at us?" Yet, there were instances of Johnnies marrying and staying in Britain – one stayed on in Scotland. Yves Gallou's widow re-married – a man from Port Talbot. Sebastien Prigent told me of instances when girls with prams had turned up at the stores asking for some young onion seller or other, who, inconsiderately had decided to go and sell his onions in some very distant corner of Britain.

On one occasion Jean-Marie, a little bit worried, told me that his wife had written to say that the money he had transferred from the bank in Cardiff had not shown up in his account in Saint-Pol. "I have paid the money into the bank here but it isn't in our bank in Brittany," he said. "I've got the receipts so I must be alright, but I worry. I'll have to go to the bank tomorrow and maybe lose half a day's selling, to argue with some buggers who are making fun of me."

At one time, when he was based in Bryn-mawr, Jean-Marie would hire a horse and cart to go selling onions. On one occasion he and his partner were going back to the stores around midnight when a man came up behind them and took one of the sticks – *ar vaz* – they used for going from door to door and hit another man who was walking along the road. "I thought that he must be dead," said Jean-Marie. "We just went away as fast as we could. The man must have been alright, though, because we never heard anything about anyone being killed." The uncertainty of a man in a strange situation in a foreign country.

Olivier said that he once had a hand-cart which he pushed around the streets of Cardiff, until he became convinced that people were stealing strings of onions from the cart. He would leave the cart on the end of the street and then take some strings on the stick. A bicycle was better because he could keep it close to him at all times – and he could ride it back to the store after he had sold all his onions.

But on one occasion someone stole his bike, onions, oilskins. All the police ever found were the pieces of wood he used to keep the onions from rubbing against the spokes of the front wheel.

A man once snatched an onion from a string Jean-Marie was carrying. "I ran after him, he dropped the onion, I picked it up, chased after him and hit him in the eye with the onion still in my fist. He must have had quite a black eye after that." Generally speaking, they were on good terms with the local people. If a lorry arrived unexpectedly with a load of onions they would go to the pub and hire anyone who was unemployed to unload the onions for them. And pay each one £5 an hour. "I never carry a hundredweight sack of onions on my back now," said Jean-Marie. "But Olivier will work with the best of them."

Some months later I met up with the two again – it was September, 1978, and I was in Brittany. As is common throughout France, the addresses given were rather imprecise. Jean-Marie's address was the worst – he had just written, J – M Cueff, Lagat Vran (The Crow's Eye), Roscoff. A few tentative enquiries proved fruitless. Olivier Bertevas's address was better, O. Bertevas, rue Chateaubriand, Saint-Pol-de-Leon. But again, all I got when I asked were vague gestures – "it's sort of in that direction". I stopped to ask for about the tenth time. A man standing in front of his house a short distance outside Saint-Pol-de-Leon. Again, I got the vague response, "in that direction" as he pointed across the fields. He was a very friendly man, in his late sixties. Then he began speaking English, English with no trace of a French accent. He had been a Johnny in Bristol. I asked him if he knew Olivier Bertevas. He said yes, but he did not know where he lived. But he knew where his partner, Shamar Cueff, lived. About a hundred yards down the road. So where was Lagat Vran? I was in Lagat Vran, more or less.

I made a mental note of the place where this man lived, got his name – Jean-Marie Prigent – and promised to call on him soon. He said he would be delighted to see me anytime. In a few minutes I arrived at Shamar Cueff's door, the Breton form of Jean-Marie is usually Yann-Bar but in these parts it became Shambar or Shamar.

Cueff's welcome would not have disappointed a long lost brother. A bottle of wine was produced and large glasses filled to the brim. This time he and Bertevas had not made the annual migration to Cardiff. "Mind, I wouldn't be surprised if Olivier would be quite happy to go if he had company – but I'm too old now," he said. We made plans for me to continue with my research. I was told to arrive just before lunch the following day and then we would set off to discover all there was to know about the Johnnies and their trade. Shamar would fix everything.

When I did arrive the following day, he was out in his large garden sowing onion seeds. These little black seeds had been kept from the 1977 harvest. He had kept them for a year and these would grow into next year's onion harvest. He would be transplanting them in February and they would be harvested in July and August of 1979. Beside him, in another bowl, were seeds from that year – 1978 – which he would keep for sowing in 1980. Did everyone have to do all this work on their knees?   What about the large farms with acres of onions?   "Everyone does it this way," said Shamar. "There are no machines for this work."

But first of all would I mind taking him shopping to a supermarket in Saint-Pol? Since I had a car, and he didn't. He suggested I might back the car up to the garage door, which he opened to reveal scores and scores of empty wine bottles. In those days we had money back on empty wine bottles. The boot of the car was virtually full by the time we had put them all in the car. It was quite an operation at the other end taking the bottles into the supermarket. He bought about a dozen bottles of wine with all the money he had back and we went back to his house for lunch – after a glass each of Ricard in a café on the way.

By the time we were back lunch was ready. Shamar's wife was gentle and quiet with a reproachful eye for Shamar's sometimes outrageous comments. Breton was the language here, and words like "Gast" peppered his language. "Gast" can mean bitch, as in Welsh but in this context it meant "prostitute". In a play by Tanguy Malmanche I once came across a particularly powerful oath – "Sapre mil gast" – sanctify a thousand whores. The house was fairly small, detached, modern with spotless tiles everywhere and like all Breton houses the workmanship was excellent.

The meal began with a tomato and onion salad, followed by pork in a very pleasant sauce with broad beans and salad and cake to finish. Washed down by a modest but very good wine.

After lunch Shamar took me look for Olivier. His detached house was at the end of a small cul-de-sac on the outskirts of Saint-Pol. It was not surprising that I had failed to find it. The windows were open but no one answered when we knocked. "Anyway, you will be able to find your way here on your own next time," said Shamar. He seemed pleased to find no one at home. That, I discovered afterwards, was because he did not get on with Madame Bertevas. I soon learnt that Shamar, even amongst the hard drinking Johnnies, had something of a reputation. There was also a lot of respect for him as a hard worker, and admiration for his eccentricity.

It was a week later when I finally got to visit Olivier in his home – a small, pleasant, semi-detached with a very large vegetable garden backing on to open fields. He had rabbit hutches in the garden although they were empty. He said that he sometimes bred rabbits and sold them to the local butchers, or killed them for his own pot. I told him that he lived in the Rhiwbina of Saint-Pol – Rhiwbina is a tidy middle-class Cardiff suburb. He smiled and approved of the description.

We walked around the garden and he complained about a mole that was playing havoc with his tiny lawn – a very small piece in the middle of a huge vegetable patch. He had spent the summer tidying other people's gardens while his wife looked after one of their grandchildren. It had been time for him to retire, he said. "Mind you, I'm prepared to bet that if I said I'd go, Shamar would be more than ready to come with me," he said. I suspected that it would not have taken much to persuade either of them to make one more trip. To freeze on cold street corners in Cardiff instead of enjoying the comfort of their nice homes. Old habits die hard. And the Johnnies were hard men with some very tough habits.

These were two men – Shamar in particular – who had dragged themselves up from very humble beginnings and were enjoying the fruits of their labour in comfortable retirement. It was another world from the shop in Bute Street. The warmth of an autumn afternoon, the smell of earth and garlic and home cooking coming from the kitchen. But this was still the same Olivier that I had known in Cardiff, quiet and shy, the same warm smile, the crooked nose. The same overalls, the same clogs and the same slippers inside the same clogs. It could have been the same badly rolled cigarette, stained brown by saliva and nicotine.

Sometimes I wondered why they put up with my company and my questioning. I think they realised they were interesting, a piece of social history that was fading away.

Chapter 6

Johnnies in England

It has often been a subject for debate - to what extent did the Johnnies like coming to Wales because, being Breton speakers, they could pick up the language? A friend, now living in Provençe, swore that he had heard Breton and Welsh speakers communicating with each other when a Breton fishing boat had got into trouble off the north coast of Cornwall. He was a helicopter pilot at the time and had flown out of Bristol to help. "They were using my radio and they were not speaking French or English, and they were certainly able to communicate with each other."

In 1985 a researcher from the BBC Education Department in London telephoned me and asked whether I could provide a transcript of a recording they had made of a Johnny Onion man from London, Jean Le Roux, speaking to some Welsh speakers from Cenarth, a village close to Newcastle Emlyn. Rather nervously I agreed. But when the tape arrived the work was a lot easier than I had anticipated. There was very little Breton on the tape, most of the conversation was in Welsh. Jean Le Roux was having no difficulty. It was obvious that he knew quite a lot of basic, conversational Welsh.

Interestingly, Jean Le Roux had never worked in Wales. His patch was Highbury in North London, and yet he knew enough Welsh to sell onions. More than that indeed. He was able to carry on a basic conversation in the language. Eight years later I met him for the first time, at his home on the outskirts of Saint-Pol-de-Leon. I tried to get him to explain to me how he knew so much Welsh as he had never been to Wales. He was very vague about the whole matter until I mentioned the people of Ceredigion in mid-Wales who at one time ran hundreds of small dairy shops in London. His eyes lit up and I realised that he had learnt all the Welsh he knew from these London Welsh shop-keepers.

It's fair to say that he had fooled the television producers from the BBC Education Department and I am ashamed to admit that I was, in my small way, an accomplice. A picture of him appeared in a handsome volume, *The Story Of English*, based on the television series, published by Faber & Faber in 1986. The caption under the picture, on page 58, says: "Jean Le Roux, a Breton, can converse in Gaelic (sic) with his Welsh cousins." Jean Le Roux could converse with his Welsh cousins because he was speaking Welsh to them!

Jean still goes on his own to sell onions in London and has a profitable side-line in speaking to journalists and to television crews – such is the fame and popularity of the Johnnies, more so that they have now become so rare.

One of my friends, a journalist in London had spent weeks trying to find him to write a feature about him for a magazine called *The Lady*. Eventually she found him in a pub in North London, for months he had spent every evening drinking with her own father!

* * *

The Bar des Johnnies looks a lot smarter these days than the place with the formica-topped tables and stools, a juke-box with lots of Elvis Presley records, and the games in the corners that I first got to know. I went there one afternoon with Jean-Marie Cueff, practising my Breton at first, then when they discovered the purpose of my visit they switched into English with obvious delight – a mixture of accents revealing where they had all been practising their trade.

It was in this bar, on the road from Notre Dame de Croaz Vaz out towards Saint-Pol, that I met an old onion seller, Alan Castell, who used to go to Liverpool. When I met him, walking was a painful process relying heavily on the aid of two walking sticks. But his conversation was lively and his memories clear. Like Jean Le Roux he was able to speak some Welsh although he had never been to Wales. "I used to sell onions to the Welsh Professor at Liverpool University in the years before the World War II. I can't remember his name except that he lived in Crosby."

Castell would take his family with him to Liverpool. "We returned every year to the same house in Formby," he said, "and my daughter would go to school in Liverpool."

Like all the Johnnies the outbreak of the war had caused great problems. "We had to return immediately and I had to sell my onions at a huge loss – I lost everything." He took a franc piece from his pocket. "That's all I had when I got home."

He talked to me about life in Roscoff after the war, a very hard time for the people of the town and the area. At one time he and a colleague would gather seaweed on the beaches and sell it to the farmers. Every one did more than one job. "We would work all night loading the ships. Then catch a few hours sleep and then out at the crack of dawn to work in the fields. As well as that we would work to repair the harbour after the damage done during the war."

He explained to me why some people in Roscoff insist that the first Johnny, Henri Olivier, was from Roscoff. "At that time Santec came under the administration of Roscoff – they were not separated administratively until 1920."

* * *

I was always struck by the accents of the Johnnies – that is, when they spoke English (or in some cases, Welsh). It was not difficult to guess where they had been selling onions – because usually they would return year after year to the same town or district. I have mentioned a man by the name of Jean-Marie Prigent – Shamar Vihan – who sold onions in Blaenavon in the valleys of Gwent. He had a cousin of the same name, who lived quite close to him on the road leading into Saint-Pol, just a little closer to the town. They looked rather alike each other, but they spoke English with completely different accents and even moved differently. The second Jean-Marie Prigent had sold onions in Bristol. He spoke English with a kind of middle-class English accent and he had a rather easy-going, slightly respectable English air about him. He had start selling onions in the city in 1920 when he was eleven years of age.

"For the first two days I went out with my father," he said. "After that I was on my own. My father put a piece of paper in my pocket with the address of the store on it in case I got lost. I was the eldest of seven children, so as soon as I was old enough to do some work it was off to England." His three bothers followed in Jean-Marie's footsteps. A few years later his father changed his patch and went to sell onions in Glasgow. His father stopped selling in 1935 and lived until 1977, when he died at the age of 96. Jean-Marie continued to sell onions in Bristol, apart from three seasons he spent in Cardiff. "I didn't like the beer in Cardiff," he said, "and I remember the pubs were shut on Sundays."

Sunday opening, or no Sunday opening, when Prigent and his fellow onion-sellers were in Brisol, Sunday morning was a time for worship. "We used to attend St Mary's Roman Catholic Church on the quay. The boss would give each one of us two pence for the collection – but we only put one on the plate and spend the other on an ice-cream cornet or a packet of cigarettes."

Although Prigent had spent only three seasons in Cardiff, he had closer links with the city. The onions from Roscoff destined for Bristol would arrive in Cardiff and he would often come to Cardiff to arrange for the load to be transported by train to Bristol. "In the years between the Wars I remembered the sailing boats bringing onions to Cardiff every three weeks and I would have to be in Cardiff to meet the boat, help unload it and get the onions transported to our base. My mother made the arrangements in Brittany, bought the onions and sent the loads over. At times we would be away from home for four to six months at a time. It was quite difficult to anticipate when the next ship would arrive in Cardiff.

"We would come over on a sailing boat. I remember I was at sea for a week once, there was no wind to swell the sails. My father was once on a sailing ship that took a month to get to Glasgow – and he suffered terribly from sea-sickness. Usually, 24 hours was long enough for those little ships to make the crossing, provided there was a fair wind."

His journeys to sell onions were long. As well as selling in Bristol he went to Bath, Trowbridge and Weston-super-mare. "I would start at 5.30 in the morning with the bike loaded with a mountain of onions and walk all the way to Weston – 22 miles. And I had to sell every string before coming back. The boss always said, 'Don't bring one onion back here, we've got plenty of onions in the store.' Years later we had a lorry and could easily travel 50 or 60 miles one way to sell our onions."

Like all the other onion men and their families the outbreak of war affected Jean-Marie Prigent. "I was in Bristol at the time and we had seven or eight tons of onions to sell. We dropped the price and sold the lot to a local merchant before returning on a ship from Southampton to Cherbourg. Some of the Johnnies stayed in England and joined the armed forces there. I know one man in Roscoff who did not return when war was declared and his family heard nothing of him until he walked into the house five years later. He had been in India and all sorts of places. He could not write home to tell his family where he was. I was not accepted for military service because of an accident I had when I was 20."

He told me how he had spent the war years working on the farms around Roscoff and recalled with pleasure the day when the Americans came – to all intents and purposes the Breton Resistance had liberated most of the country before the Americans arrived. "I was working in a field when I saw them coming. I asked if anyone had cigarettes and someone threw a packet to me. Another one asked if I liked chocolate and before I could say a word I had a large piece in my hand. I asked if anyone could sell me a pair of boots. A black American sat down beside me, he took his boots off and offered them to me. 'Are they OK?' he asked. 'They're fine,' I replied. 'How much do you want for them?' 'Five hundred francs?' he suggested. I gave him the money gladly. I had worn nothing but clogs since the beginning of the war. Clogs are fine in the winter in the cold and wet, but they are much too hot to wear in summer."

Prigent returned to Bristol after the war but his annual migration did not last long. He went over for the last time in 1951. After the war he would take his load of onions by boat to Portsmouth and from there to Bristol by lorry. "We used a primus stove to cook in the store. But they were difficult days because of the food rationing – there was not much meat. Of course, we had our ration books like everyone else."

He said that he once got into difficulty because he was taking many packets of tea back to Brittany. As he and his fellow workers rarely drank tea they were taking their tea ration home to their wives. But the customs men would not believe their story – they were convinced the Johnnies had bought the tea on the black market!

After retiring from onion selling, Prigent worked as an agent for a local merchant buying vegetables from farmers in the Roscoff and Saint-Pol-de-Leon area. "The children don't want to follow on in the old trade – I have a daughter who is a teacher in Brest and a son in Paris. The young people want to go to Paris – they don't want to stay on the farms around here. They get better money by going away."

* * *

I sat outside Saint Barbe's chapel. It was a warm September afternoon in 1978. I have never been inside the chapel and I was thinking about something Jean-Marie Cueff had told me – how he and his friends would come and put money in the collection box in the hope that this somehow would ensure their safe return. A man, he looked to be in middle age, sat nearby. "You are welcome to go inside and look around the place," he said. I was about to say "Thanks, but where do I get a key?" when, to my disappointment, I realised that he was referring to the Societé Langouste buildings below us – not Saint Barbe's chapel behind us. I thanked him and said I would take advantage of the opportunity when I had a little more time. To the east of us a long cargo boat, low in the water, throbbed its way with a load of sand up the estuary towards Morlaix. Looking in the other direction it was obvious why it had been necessary to create a new, deep water, harbour in Roscoff. The tide was far out and there was no hope that the most shallow boat could weave a way out to sea from the old port at that hour. The lobster pots piled high on the quay indicated that old industries still thrived in and around the old port.

I decided to draw the man into a conversation. His name was François Gueguen and I quickly learnt that he was much older than he looked – he was 76 – and he had been a Johnny for the best part of his life. We walked together along the old harbour towards the centre of the town, he pushing his bicycle. It was one of those sturdy bicycles with a small engine mounted against the handlebars, which were popular in France at one time. The bike was powered by small wheel which rotated against the tyre of the front wheel. They were able to wind up to a fair turn of speed while, no doubt, wearing the tyre down very quickly as well.

He had started selling onions in Scotland with his father in 1913. He was 11 years of age at the time. As we walked back along the harbour he told me about the years he had spent in the trade. "It was from there, the near side of that quay that the onions were loaded," he said. "We were at the mercy of the winds and the tide in those days. I remember the ships came mostly from Treguier and Paimpol. They would sail from here full of onions and return loaded with coal."

He recalled the years of hardship – his father had been killed in 1916. After the war Gueguen had returned to Britain to sell onions with an uncle. Among the places they had been based were Kendall and Middlesborough. "I remember seeing horses being led out of the pits in Durham in 1926 – they were blind as bats.

"I would carry 20 strings of onions – that was more than a 100 pounds – on the stick on my back. I was just thankful that it got lighter as the day went on." We walked on, past Mary Stuart's house, until we got to the church of Notre Dame de Croaz Vaz with its two stone canons carved from one of the towers, intended to scare the "perfidious Albion" away in the old days. Since then houses and hotels have been built between the church and the sea, so it's hard to judge to what extent they would have been a deterrent.

* * *

I have already mentioned François Keriven who had been at first a reluctant seller in Hull. How he had to be bribed with pieces of chocolate or threatened with a good hiding to leave the store and go selling onions. His nephew, also named François Keriven, still goes to sell onions in Leeds. He is short man, lively, with a gruff voice. Both had worked together in a number of towns in the north of England – Darlington, Hull, Leeds ... If the Johnnies who went to Wales or Scotland felt an affinity with those Celtic countries, the two Kerivens were full of praise for the warm hearted, welcoming people of the north of England. It is obvious that the younger of the two has many friends amongst the English. "After a day out selling I'll have a wash, shave, tidy myself and go out to the pub for a pint with my English friends."

He once showed me a remarkable document, a document that proved that his father had come over to Southampton in 1916, at the height of the Great War, to sell onions. Not a passport as such, but a permit to travel to Britain. It had been stamped in Southampton and the date was quite clear. I never heard any mention of another Johnny coming over during that period. It would, I suppose, have been possible – if risky – since the battles of the First War were fought in northern France and Belgium. The onion men were always ready to take a risk, François Keriven's father was obviously no exception.

* * *

To many in Roscoff's respectable circles, Saik Mevel was the doyen of the Johnnies. To the Johnnies themselves he was le chanteur. During the years he spent selling onions in London he would supplement his earnings by singing in the cabarets of London's West End. One of his fellow onion sellers once said to me, "he never sold many onions, but he did very well with his singing."

110

He was born in 1899 and the last time I saw and spoke to him w in the Café Ty Pierre in Roscoff. It was 1991 and he was leading tl singing to be recorded for a programme on the onion sellers for th Welsh television channel, S4C. Saik had been a source of many folk songs for the folk choir Mouez Rosko, and I remember meeting his daughter who was a member of that choir. She, too, had a fine voice.

A few years before that I sat in his house – named Summerfield – listening to him sing the anthem of the Johnnies, *Good onions, very cheap*, a Breton song with a few phrases of English thrown in. He also sang *Bro Goz va Zadou*, Brittany's national anthem, an adaptation of Wales's national anthem, *Hen Wlad Fy Nhadau* (Land of my Fathers). "I love watching Wales play rugby – on the television of course – so that I can hear the crowd sing that song at the start of the match," he said. "I can join in and sing until the windows rattle."

But in the cabarets of London's West End, it was not the songs of his native land that he sang but the popular arias from the operas, such as *Your tiny hand is frozen* from *La Bohème*. He even had his own music tutor in London. "He taught me to sing with my brain, not from my heart," he said. His daughter told me that Saik was also a poet and he would write Breton words for songs from other countries, which were then sung by Mouez Rosko.

Like many of the onion men he was a man of wide cultural interests. A copy of a painting of London Bridge by Bernard Buffet was hanging in his lounge and a still life original by Cecil Kennedy – given to him by the artist himself. "In every one of Kennedy's paintings there is ladybird in some corner or other," he said, pointing to the one in this particular painting. "I sold onions to Kennedy for years – he was one of my best customers."

Saik Mevel began selling onions with his father in Grimsby in 1913. He was 14 at the time. The following year he was about to leave Roscoff when war was declared and he was stopped in time. He started selling again in Croydon in 1923, and between the two wars, London and its suburbs was his market. "At the time there were 150 Johnnies in London, Essex and Surrey alone." Even in the early 1970s he estimated that there were about 50 Johnnies working in the south-east of England.

After World War II Saik Mevel settled around Romford and Hornchurch and to the end of his life he considered the people of Essex to be amongst the best on earth. He came over for the last time in 1974 – at the age of 75.

He, too, was in Britain when war was declared in 1939. "I was selling onions in Leytonstone and I had to return immediately. I joined the Fire Brigade in Paris and that's where I stayed until 1945."

* * *

I have mentioned Jean Le Roux who still comes over to Highbury in London. Paul Caroff and his wife spend a few months every winter in Poole. There were two companies in Poole as late as the 1970s – the Caroff company and that of François Danielou. When Danielou retired he went to work on Brittany Ferries.

Guillaume Seité, now 89, stopped going to Bristol three years ago. He kept on selling despite one terrible experience. One night in January 1978 his colleague, Eugène Cabioc'h, never returned to the store. He was 68. Seité told me that it was believed that he fell into the docks on the way home in a fog. His body was never found.

Seité tells a funny story about selling onions when he was very young and his knowledge of English very shaky. "And what's your name, little fellow?" a potential customer asked him. "Two bob," he replied. (Younger readers may not know that "two bob" is the equivalent of 10p in today's currency.)

Chapter 7

Disasters and Difficulties

The Johnnies were fortunate that their trade was established in favourable times. Their numbers and the tonnage of onions imported into Britain grew steadily from 1828 to 1900. From the point of view of trade, conditions seemed to be on their side. But over the decades a series of disasters eventually led to the decline of their trade – a decline that was almost, if not yet, terminal. Disasters at sea were the worst to hit the Johnnies and their communities.

Channel Queen

The first of these was the shipwreck of the *Channel Queen* about 5 am on Tuesday, February 1, 1898, near Guernsey. The *Channel Queen* was a steamer, built in Middlesborough in 1895, and owned by the Plymouth, Channel Islands and Brittany Co. A 385 ton boat, 177 feet long and 24 feet wide which sailed between Plymouth and Saint-Brieuc.

The *Channel Queen* left Plymouth in thick fog at 11pm on Monday, January 31. During the night the fog became thicker. According to what one Johnny, who was saved, told a reporter from *Matin* in Guernsey, there were 48 passengers on the boat, 44 of them were onion sellers on their way home from Falmouth and Exeter. "There were two companies of onion sellers," he said. "The first consisted of 18 men and the second of 36. We were returning to Brittany after a stay in England of anything between a month and six months ... the *Channel Queen* had a crew of 19 and a total of 48 passengers, three of whom travelled first class.

"The ship had made its journey unhindered. Some of us were sleeping in the stores, others were out on the bridge, when suddenly the engines stopped. It was about 5am.

"We hit a rock. The water penetrated the hold, and it was evident the vessel was sinking rapidly. The two lifeboats were put to sea. The first capsized and the seven passengers, who had got into it, clung desperately to the keel but could not be saved by the other boat. The second lifeboat, with nine of our compatriots, made it to the shore.

"The local fishermen, informed of the disaster, came directly to our aid, but the rocks were so dangerous that the rescuers had to keep their distance. They threw ropes and lifebelts to us. During this time the water swept over the port side and with it some of our compatriots who disappeared for ever. One wave plucked a child from the arms of its mother."

According to the captain, a man named Collings, the total number of passengers was 40, but as can be seen later in the disaster of the *Hilda*, the authorities were never very sure exactly how many people were on board their ships – apart from those who travelled first class. Collings told *Matin*: "About 5am the *Channel Queen* hit a rock, rebounded heavily and rested stuck on the Black Rock, a mile from the coast and half a mile from the Great Havre." Collings did not abandon the ship until the water was almost up to his armpits.

At low tide, part of the ship could be seen, but at high tide only the tips of the mast could be seen. A few days later a clearer picture emerged. By February 3 it was evident that 24 had died in the disaster, eighteen of them had French or Breton names. They were the Johnnies. Amongst the 18 onion sellers who lost their lives were five youngsters – aged 10, 13, 14, 17 and 19. The steamer *L'Aber* arrived on February 6 to take those who had been saved to Saint Brieuc.

As can be expected there was grave concern in Roscoff and Saint-Pol-de-Leon as families waited for news of their relatives. Lives had been lost, so too were substantial sums of money on which many Breton families depended until next year's migration. Neither the passengers nor the money they carried on their persons were insured. The loss, in every way, was a tragedy. Such disasters did not inspire confidence in those who considered taking up, or continuing, the trade of the Johnnies.

Other ships sank: *Saint-Joseph* (1902), *Le Chouan* (1905), *Water Lily* (1909), *Le Hermann* (1925) … but in very case no lives were lost – just the cargo. Between July 20 and July 30, 1908, three dundees ran aground on the rocks between Bloscon and L'Île de Batz, which proved that the old port of Roscoff was one of the most dangerous on the whole of France's coastline. Often the ships would be overloaded making them difficult to handle. On other occasions salt water would get into the hold and ruin the onions.

The *Hilda* disaster

A little before midnight on Saturday, November 18, 1905, the *Hilda* sank on her way into Saint-Malo. It was the worst disaster in the history of the Johnnies – 125 people were drowned, 74 of them were onion sellers.

The *Hilda* was an 848 ton steamer owned by the London and South Western Railway Company on its way from Southampton to Saint-Malo and as in the case of the *Channel Queen*, husbands, fathers, sons, brothers as well as large sums of money were lost.

The steamer left Southampton at 10pm on Friday, November 17. According to Lloyd's Register of Shipping she carried a total of 131 persons, 79 of whom were Breton onion sellers, and a crew of 28 under the command of Captain William Gregory. She had been due to leave Southampton at 8.15pm, but was delayed by heavy fog and then had to anchor off Yarmouth, Isle of Wight, until dawn. The fog cleared and the ship sailed until at mid-day it ran into a series of stormy, squally showers of sleet and snow and heavy seas. By 6pm the *Hilda* had arrived at the Chenal de Petite Porte on the way into Saint-Malo. Once more the wind increased and the ship ran into another blinding snow storm. In the hope that the storm would subside the captain put out to sea to wait for the weather to clear and an opportunity to sail safely into the harbour. He waited for another five or six hours. Then, at some time he must have decided to try to get into the harbour – possibly because of the complaints of some of his passengers.

Just before midnight the *Hilda* struck a reef known as the Pierres des Portes. The first lifeboat was lowered immediately but it was smashed before it hit the water and before the other lifeboats could be got away the ship broke in two. The stern portion, where most of the passengers were, sank immediately.

Reuters News Agency reported from Saint-Servan in Brittany:
The majority of the crew and passengers were asleep in their bunks when the *Hilda* struck, and so there was no time for everybody to come on deck and help lower the boats. Two boats were, however, lowered and one of them has arrived here. The second has been picked up empty at Saint-Cast, where 13 bodies have been washed ashore. It is supposed they belonged to the *Hilda*. Four more bodies have been picked up at the scene of the disaster by steamers sent from Saint-Malo and bought here this afternoon. Four of the men

115

saved are onion sellers and the fifth belonged to the crew. The top of the *Hilda's* funnel and one mast are visible at low water.

The sole survivor from the crew of 28, Able Seaman James Grinter, recalled his experiences to a *Daily Mail* reporter in Saint-Malo, an account of which appeared in the paper's edition of November 27:

... there was a terrible snowstorm and suddenly a horrible shock went through the ship followed by the sound of friction. I think that it was about midnight.

Within minutes I was on the bridge. In spite of the darkness I could see the spiky rocks. The captain ordered the boats to be put to sea. The ship rolled terribly and with every movement ran onto rocks .... The French onion sellers helped to put the lifebelts on the women. As the ship leaked I was struck by the apparent calm of everyone. We were in a vortex of snow as the ship sank. I was flung into the rigging and I climbed the great mast with the mate. There were about 25 people in the rigging when the boat sank.

"The mate held on until 6am and then fell headlong into the water ... At day-break we could see the rocks and I saw the *Ada*.

The *Ada* was a steamer belonging to the same company as the *Hilda*. The *Ada* should have sailed from Saint-Malo on Friday night but because of the storm and the danger of colliding with the *Hilda* in the channel the captain postponed sailing until day-break on Sunday, November 19. The *Ada* sailed at 8am and in a short time the captain, through his telescope, witnessed the catastrophe. He saw the ship's masts on the Pierres des Portes which are some four miles from Saint-Malo and slightly less than half a mile from a lighthouse called the Grand Jardin. He realised instantly that it was the *Hilda* and ordered the lifeboats be put to sea immediately.

One of the Johnnies who survived, Olivier Caroff of Roscoff, descibed the events in greater detail than Grinter, with less emphasis on calm and more on the panic. He was quoted in the *Chronique* of Saint-Malo, November 24):

The memory of that terrible night is a nightmare. I had been asleep before the disaster but I woke suddenly because of the cold. I got up. It was pitch black, I couldn't see further than four metres. I walked towards the bridge where I saw the captain giving orders. 'Filthy weather' I said to a passing sailor; we must have been close to Saint-Malo, but I couldn't see the lighthouse.

A little later, I think I glimpsed a glimmer of light. The Great Jardin lighthouse is green, white and red. The boat siren whistled violently, the alarm bell sounded. I thought of returning to my bed when a tremendous shock went through the boat and hurled me backwards. I got up and ran towards the stern. I ran into the mast. The ship was sinking. I started climbing the mast.

Then I saw people running wildly. Men were climbing all around me. I hastened to get up there, the higher the better. There was terrible cracking, a rumbling sound, the centre of the ship disappeared and sank. I heard shrieks that made my blood run cold.

There were a score of us on the mast. Every so often one of us fell off. The cold was getting to me. How long did I pass thus? I cannot say. When day came, I saw the smoke, a black mass. It was the *Ada*! Life! The boatswain's mate, Morel, arrived with sailors in a boat. I don't remember any more until I woke up in hospital in their warm sheets. That morning I gave thanks that I was alive."

Maurice Tuloup-Lorilleux in his *Histoire Generale de Saint-Malo* pieced together the following description of events:

The snow storm was violent, one could not see beyond five metres … Captain Gregory who had been in command of the ship for many years, certainly knew the danger and wished to stay well off Cazembre, but the passengers who had suffered from the heavy weather were so insistent that they be taken into Saint-Malo that against his better judgement, he decided to cross these at the best of times very dangerous channels. In such weather this was an extremely treacherous crossing. It was midnight. The winking white, green and red light of the Tour du Grand Jardin could no longer be seen, neither the winking white of the Noires of Saint-Malo nor the Balue which indicated the route to follow. He took the wrong route.

His ship ripped itself on the rocks and the furious waves shattered it in two. The front part rested on the Roc des Plates which was the main danger in that channel. The other part sank. The passengers had all put on their life jackets. They floated thus as the fury of the waves carried them towards the shore. The freezing cold did not spare them. The following morning, at Saint-Cast, 69 corpses, kept upright by their lifejackets, were carried to the shore on the current. It was a sight which struck terror into the hearts of the local people.

The *Daily Mail* correspondent in Saint-Malo on Tuesday, November 21, wrote:

Returning by the wreck this evening at low tide, I was able to visit it, for the front part, completely broken off, is perched prow upwards on a jagged rock. It was evidently steaming full speed at the time of the accident. Ten yards to the left of the rock and the *Hilda* would have steamed through an open channel.

In Saint-Cast on the same day, a *Daily Mail* special correspondent described the scenes in that small town:

The scene at Saint-Cast beggars description, so heartrending is it. All the bodies have now been placed in the old church, whose door is draped in black with the French and English flags lying at half-mast. The church bell is tolling continually, and Mass succeeds Mass. The old church is full of flowers and wreaths, and is crowded with relations and friends of the victims.

The grief of the Breton women is terrible to witness. One of them beats her breast, continually calling out, 'Ma Doue! Ma Doue!' and bending down to kiss the face of her only son. One woman, on entering the church, recognising three brothers and her husband, fainted away.

One can hear nothing but wailing and cries of distress. One man, half mad with grief, is calling to his brother – a corpse – and wringing him by the hand.

Many are washing the faces of the dead with holy water. The Cure is consoling the relations, but they are all half mad with grief. In front of the church are roughly-constructed coffins scattered about waiting for the identifications to be completed.

No more bodies have yet been discovered. The wind has changed and local sailors think they are being carried out to sea, and may not be found for days. I have inspected the belongings of the victims, and nearly every watch stopped at a quarter to twelve. Only one watch had stopped at 11.30.

The *Daily Mail* correspondent in Saint-Malo described a visit he had just made to Saint-Cast as "one of the saddest scenes in life." He continued:

Be it said to the credit of the inhabitants of this out-of-the-way place that, although most of the corpses had sums varying from £25 to £200 in English gold in belts round their waists, and although even in some cases the gold was found scattered, it was gathered and laid on the body to which it was nearest. The worthy Bretons scorned to rob the dead.

When the lifeboats of the *Ada* arrived at the scene of the disaster, only five survivors were found, all clinging, cramped with cold to the *Hilda's* rigging. Four of them were Johnnies – Olivier Caroff of Roscoff, Paul-Marie Penn of Cleder, Tanguy Laot of Cleder and Jean-Louis Rozec of Plouzevede. The other survivor was the sailor, James Grinter. Jean-Louis Mouster of La Feuillée was picked up later on a nearby islet where he had been walking non-stop in an effort to get some warmth into his body. He had seen his brother-in-law being plucked away to his death by the waves.

The other survivors had similar stories to tell. Penn had climbed the rigging with a 14 year-old boy, Calarnou of Cleder, on his back. The teenager died of exposure. Another Cleder man, whose surname was Velly, also died from the cold.

So, exactly how many Johnnies were there on the *Hilda*? According to the Lloyd's Register of Shipping there was a total of 131 people on the ship; 79 of them were onion sellers, 24 other passengers and a crew of 28. At the time it proved a difficult task to discover exactly how many people had been on the ship. *The Times* correspondent in Southampton on November 19 telegraphed that "the crew numbered 26; and there were 20 ordinary passengers and 54 onion men." As the majority of the Johnnies were travelling third-class there was no list of their names. *Reuter's News Agency* reported from Saint-Servan on the same day that 123 lives had been lost. At Saint-Malo it was being estimated that there were 60 onion sellers on the ship. But it was not until the bodies were floating ashore in frightening numbers that an accurate assessment of the magnitude of the tragedy could be made. It was announced on November 21 that the sea had yielded 60 bodies on the beach of Saint-Cast, 15 in Plevenou, two in Saint-Jacut, and five in Saint-Malo. Among the bodies discovered on the beach of Saint-Cast was that of Captain William Gregory. On November 22 came further news from Saint-Cast that on board the *Hilda* had been "besides the first and second class passengers and crew, 82 onion merchants, all of Finistère. 77 are dead of whom 44 are from the single commune of Cleder."

At Roscoff, no one knew exactly the number of onion-selling companies who had embarked on the *Hilda* in Southampton. Many of the Johnnies had written in their letters that they would be sailing either on Saturday or Sunday. The uncertainty and confusion increased the consternation. Representatives from Roscoff were sent to Saint-Malo to seek information as regards who had lost their lives.

Rumours spread like wildfire. It was believed that the Johnnies were carrying large sums in gold about their persons and as a result the authorities gave orders for strict surveillance of the coast to prevent any plundering. One rumour claimed that some of the Johnnies had as much as 50,000 francs on them – but it was discovered that the figure was between 2,800 and 15,000 francs.

Identifying the corpses caused the saddest moments of all. A Madame Kerbiriou from Roscoff found the bodies of her two sons, Eugène, aged 13, and Jean, aged 17. A Madame Calarnou died on November 25 when she found the remains of her 14 year old son. The bodies of two Pichon brothers were identified by their sister. Later she found her husband, too, among the dead. On the Monday following the disaster two young men from Roscoff walked in their clogs all the way to Saint-Cast to see if they would find their father's body among the corpses. They did not find his remains there and they continued to Saint-Malo where they arrived at 6pm on the Wednesday. They had walked 184 kilometres in 48 hours. The poor men did not have the money to travel by train, but they did not hesitate to undertake the journey to try and give their father a proper burial.

By the evening of November 22 all the bodies that had been recovered had been identified – except two, an English woman and an onion seller known only as Guillaume. All 20 members of J. M. Calarnou's company from Cleder had been lost. Twelve of them were from Cleder, six from Plouescat and two from Plougoulm. All 13 members of Paul Jaouen's company were lost – five were from Plouescat, five from Cleder and three others whose place of birth is no longer known. Of Louis Quiviger's company, 14 were drowned and two survived. Again the majority were from Cleder. Louis Tanguy of Sibiril was drowned as were his sons Guillaume, aged 25, Claude, who was 18, and François, aged 14. The company of the Pichon brothers from Roscoff consisted of 17 members – seven from Roscoff, three from Sibiril, three from Le Feuillée, two from Saint-Pol-de-Leon, one from Plouenan and one from Plougoulm. Of these, 14 were lost and one was saved. Another two had not embarked at Southampton. One had suddenly felt a desire to have a look at the town before sailing and missed the boat – for three days his parents believed that he was dead. The other had gone celebrating and was picked up by the police in a drunken state and thrown in the cells for the night. He was grateful to the Southampton police for the rest of his life.

Cleder was the place that suffered worst of all. Of the total number that drowned, 44 were from that commune, more than half the total of those lost. In those days there was no insurance and many families as well as losing loved ones had lost a year's earnings and were facing a period of terrible poverty.

A number of funds were launched, one by the Mayor of Southampton, another by the French Chamber of Trade in London. Students in Rennes organised a concert and *Le Gaulois*, a newspaper, launched an appeal which raised around 13,055 francs.

According to the weekly paper, *La Resistance,* of Morlaix, there were in Britain that season 58 companies and a total of 1152 Johnnies. The biggest company, according to the paper, was that of Paul Grall with 41 sellers although it did not say where that company was based.

After such a shattering disaster it was not surprising that there was a considerable decrease in the number of Johnnies who went to Britain the following year. Many a head of the family stopped and the wives of those who carried on lived in fear until they had heard that their husbands had arrived safely in Britain – and likewise when they were expecting them home.

By 1907 the numbers were back up to 1,200 and 1,300 by 1909. If the loss of loved ones still ached in their hearts, poverty and hunger drove them back year after year.

Transferring money through a bank in Britain to the *Banque de Bretagne* in Saint-Pol-de-Leon did not become common practice until 1921. Indeed some Johnnies did not take advantage of such facilities until 1948.

Aliens Act of 1905

Earlier in 1905 the Johnnies had come face to face with another problem – a very minor irritant compared to the disaster of the *Hilda* but one that had an effect on them for decades. No more than 20 Johnnies were allowed to disembark from one ship in ports which were not ports of immigration. Nevertheless, there were instances of ships landing numbers greater than that – in Swansea on July 24, 1905, 23 Johnnies were allowed to disembark; four days later a ship with 22 Johnnies on board docked in Swansea and a day later, on July 29, 34 Johnnies were allowed to land in the same port.

On July 27, 1905, a ship docked in Swansea with 27 Johnnies on board. In each case they were allowed to come ashore. In fact, the French authorities in Brest were far more concerned about this Act than the British port authorities. Later when the law was tightened there were stories about ships landing Johnnies on remote beaches before heading for some small port with the onions and the regulation number of Johnnies. The two groups of Johnnies would then meet up at an agreed place and time. No doubt the Breton sailors knew where this could be done in reasonable safety – smuggling was in their blood, after all.

The Aliens Act was an irritant rather than a serious problem. The ships could always sail to a larger port, or the Johnnies could cross over on their own – a train to Calais, for example, a ferry to Dover and then on by train to join the rest of the company wherever they would be spending the season.

The Great War

In spite of the disaster of the *Hilda* the trade of the Johnnies was thriving again in no time at all and 1,000 were crossing to Britain every season in the years leading up to 1914 – the year the Great War began. The numbers tended to fluctuate with the size of the crop. The better the harvest, the greater the number of Johnnies.

The Great War was declared at the worst possible time for the Johnnies who had already left Roscoff – and they were the ones who travelled furthest. I have already dealt with that episode in Jean Berthou's reminiscences in an earlier chapter.

It should not be forgotten that 250,000 young men from Brittany lost their lives in that futile war – a far greater percentage than from any other of France's provinces. This affected the Roscoff and Saint-Pol-de-Leon areas just as it affected other parts of Brittany. And, of course, the trade ceased for five years. (In spite of the very interesting fact – see the previous chapter – that François Keriven's father was selling onions in 1916. François was not able to explain that unusual occurrence to me and I am not aware of any other Johnny having made the crossing in that period.)

Problems in the Thirties

The Johnnies took up their trade again with enthusiasm after the Great War and by the end of the Twenties and the early Thirties they had reached their "golden age". By now 1,500 men – and amongst them some women – from Roscoff and the surrounding area were spending their winters in Britain. In the period between 1927 and 1931 the area was also exporting between 9,700 and 10,000 tons of onions every season.

In 1929 the Department for the British Merchant Navy was beginning to take a tougher line on the number of onion sellers who were allowed to cross over on ships carrying onions. From now on no more than a dozen onion sellers were allowed to travel on a ship carrying onions – regardless of the size of the ship. The Aliens Act of 1905 was being enforced with renewed vigour.

In 1931 Britain was in financial difficulties. The Buy British movement was established with the intention, as the name suggests, of persuading people to buy British produce. In conversations I had with many former Johnnies it was obvious that this movement had had some effect on their trade – some more than others. Devaluing the pound was far more serious. Nothing pleased the Johnnies more than a strong pound against a weak franc. So when the pound was devalued during the 1931/2 season this was a serious blow to the Johnnies.

Within a year they were to suffer another blow from British protectionism. An import tax of 10 per cent was placed on produce being brought into Britain. (More favourable conditions were imposed on British Commonwealth countries under the Ottawa Agreement.) All this had the effect of decreasing the number of Johnnies in the companies, and now, instead of one company chartering a ship entirely for itself, one ship might bring onions over for as many as 30 much smaller companies. While there were 58 companies in 1905, by 1934 the number of companies had increased to 93, although the number of Johnnies had decreased substantially.

Because of these difficulties the tonnage exported to Britain went down from 10,000 in 1931 to 3,245 in 1932. By 1933 the tonnage had decreased further to 2,786. In 1936 the tonnage exported had increased to 4,500. Things were definitely looking better in 1937, and the sellers were able to seek higher prices, but due to the low prices in 1936 the farmers had planted fewer onions and only 2,203 tons were exported to Britain. It would have been possible to sell much, much more but there were not enough onions to sell.

In 1932 the Colorado Beetle plagued parts of the continent, and although the beetle never came near Brittany, let alone the Roscoff area – vegetables, including Breton onions, were not allowed to be sold on the islands of Jersey or Guernsey. The Johnnies did not enjoy the same happy relationship with the inhabitants of these islands as they did with the people of Britain. There was trouble, for example, between the Johnnies and vegetable growers in Jersey in 1899. Few companies, however, went to Jersey and Guernsey.

World War II

As in the Great War, World War II stopped the trade of the onion men. But the after-effects of the second war were much worse. During 1939 – 45 the British Government had urged their farmers to increase production. After the War the British Government continued with this policy of encouraging the farmers to continue with their high level of food production and to keep imports to a minimum. Farmers were paid £2 an acre for ploughing rough grazing land and draining and cultivating wetlands.

The Ministry of Food then created further barriers to those who wanted to import foreign fruits and vegetables – a way of rewarding the farmers who had seen Britain through the war years, perhaps. This was done by prohibiting companies importing goods into Britain from retailing those goods. This would create a "middle-man" who would want his share of the proceeds and thus, artificially, increase the price of the product by the time it got to the shop. Thus giving the British farmers an advantage.

Prohibiting companies from importing and retailing hit at the very heart of the Johnnies trade. Not only did they export their onions into Britain and then sell them from door to door, many of them also grew the onions they sold! They were producing, exporting and selling their onions directly to their customers. This new trade barrier was going to destroy the whole tradition, trade and way of life of the Johnnies.

The Bretons claim that the Leonards are the most headstrong of all the Bretons. And the people of Roscoff are said to be the most determined of all the Leonards. They needed all that determination in the months ahead. They immediately launched a campaign to save the Johnnies. The key person was François Mazeas, born in 1911, and who had been an onion seller in Bradford before World War II. He was better educated than most of the Johnnies and could speak and write English fluently. And he proved himself an able leader at this difficult time.

The London Government refused his first application on behalf of the Johnnies at the end of 1945. But he refused to be beaten. He went to Paris and for a fortnight he knocked on the doors of the *Ministère de l'Agriculture*, the *Ministère des Finances et des Affaires Économiques* and the *Centre National du Commerce Extérieur* (CNCE). As is the way of petty bureaucrats the world over he was sent from office to office, from floor to floor, from department to department. No one in Paris had ever heard of the men from Brittany who, since 1828, had gone to sell their onions in Britain! Eventually, in the CNCE, the department responsible for offering services and advice to farmers he found someone prepared to listen. It was arranged that he should go and speak to a trade counsellor in the French Embassy in London. In 22 Hans Place, London, Mazeas met the trade attaché, a man by the name of Mareschal. Mareschal promised his support and that he, personally, would go to the offices of all the appropriate British Government Ministries to speak on behalf of the Johnnies. He kept his word and proved himself to be one of the most genuine, efficient and determined supporters of the Johnnies. Lobbying of Parliament in Britain, and no doubt in other countries, has become a huge – and by now a somewhat discredited – practice. Mareschal and Mazeas were lobbying Members of Parliament in London long before corporations began paying large sums to people to lobby on their behalf. But if the junior officials in the Paris ministries had never heard of the Johnnies, every Member of Parliament in London knew – personally – at least one onion seller. This fact was to prove very important.

Fortunately for the Johnnies the onion harvest in Britain in the summer of 1946 was a disaster. The Johnnies were invited to export as many tons of onions as they possibly could. It was an unexpected request and the men of Roscoff, Saint-Pol-de-Leon and the surrounding villages responded swiftly and in the middle of February 1947 they exported many, many tons of onions to Britain. They were not allowed to sell their onions in the traditional way – but the door was partly opened.

Also, the British Government, through its Ministry of Food was talking to the Johnnies. The first thing the Ministry of Food insisted on was that the onion sellers should form an association. As a result the *Association des vendeurs d'oignons de Roscoff et de sa région* was formed. It was not an unreasonable request – the British Ministry of Food could not be expected to negotiate with a group of independently minded determined individuals. The association was formed and it was the responsibility of *Ar Master* to pay his own fee and for every one in his company. Every onion seller was issued with a card that was acknowledged by the police and other authorities in Britain. The membership fee fluctuated from year to year. It was natural that the first president of the association was François Mazeas.

After the association had been properly established in a manner acceptable to the British Ministry of Food, the Johnnies were allowed to sell once more in their time-honoured way. But there were restrictions – to ensure advantages for the onion growers of Britain. These were a few of them:

1. Exports to Britain in the following season (1947-48) would be limited to 2,500 tons.

2. Licences to sell were not to be issued to anyone who had not been an onion seller before the war.

3. The Johnnies could not sell onions for more than four and a half pence a pound (about 2 pence in British decimal coinage). Every Johnny had to have a spring scale (*Eur stillen*) with him at all times which was in accordance with the Weights and Measures department. He would have to produce it if asked to do so by an Inspector from the Department of Weights and Measures.

4. The onions that the Johnnies sold in Britain had to have been harvested in France (!) by the seller or by his employer. No onion seller was allowed to buy onions, or any other similar products – such as

garlic and shallots – to sell in Britain.

Any onion seller caught selling his merchandise for more than four and a half pence a pound or who contravened any of the conditions stipulated by the Ministry was liable to be prosecuted and have to appear before a British court.

There were other restrictions, such as when the onion sellers could export. They could not export onions between the middle of August and the middle of November. So it was a rush to get as many onions as possible harvested and ready to go before the middle of August. The best part of the crop would be harvested from the middle to the end of August. This, again, was to ensure an advantage for the British onion growers. However, the onion sellers of that small corner of north-western Brittany were much better placed than onion growers in the rest of France – or other countries in Europe for that matter. In December 1948 onion growers in every part of France were in a dreadful situation – they had nowhere to sell their produce. The only region able to sell its onions was that area around Roscoff and Saint-Pol-de-Leon – thanks to a very special relationship which had existed for over a century between the Johnnies and the people of Britain. And the determination of those onion sellers to continue that relationship. The situation, nevertheless, was far from ideal and the pound was devalued in 1949 – the Johnnies were always dismayed whenever that happened.

By this time all the companies of onion sellers were taking advantage of banking facilities to transfer their earnings to Brittany – usually to the Banque de Bretagne in Saint-Pol. Old warehouses were not the safest of places to keep their money, although I never heard of Johnnies being robbed of their money. And there were risks to taking money back with them as the *Hilda* disaster showed.

Mazeas and Mareschal fought on to get all the restrictions imposed in the post-war period lifted. In 1950, the only restriction that remained was the one that prevented the Johnnies from exporting onions to Britain between August 15 and November 15. This was giving the British onion growers a big advantage over the Bretons.

Eventually, by 1954, after much negotiating the Johnnies were enjoying the same freedom as they had before the war. All that was left was the duty the Johnnies had to pay when they brought their onions into the British ports. But that already existed before 1939. The obstinate men of Roscoff had won their battle – but had they lost the war? Was it too late?

In 1956 Mazeas had an accident which did serious damage to his leg and he gave up selling onions. He continued as president of the *Association des vendeurs d'oignons* until 1958. He was the "star" of a BBC documentary, *Onion Johnny*, produced by Stephen Hearst which was broadcast in 1960 – a classic film that won an international award in a festival in Canada.

The British Government had nothing against the Johnnies as such. The total tonnage of onions they brought with them into Britain had very little effect on British agriculture. The Johnnies suffered from, and fought against, the effects of a law created to safeguard British agriculture and barriers raised to prohibit imports from such countries as Spain and Holland. These countries sold far greater quantities of onions to Britain than the Johnnies. (See the table in the appendix.) When the law was made no one had thought of the traditional, original and colourful Johnnies. The miracle was that they managed to cut their way through the wall of bureaucracy built to defend British agriculture. It was an indication of their immense determination, and the affection which the people of Britain had for them, that they succeeded.

But was it the beginning of the end for the Johnnies? The 1939-45 war and the subsequent uncertainties were to prove damaging. The numbers were down to 250 in 1948 and were as low as 75 in 1949. In Roscoff there was plenty of work – re-building after the ravages of war, for example.

The trade of the Johnnies picked up in the 1950s. By 1955 there were 352 Johnnies in 43 centres but after that their numbers continued to decline. By 1970 their numbers had dwindled to 144 working out of 80 different centres. Obviously, at least 20 were coming over and working on their own. In the 1970s many of the onion sellers I had got to know were giving up.

Their trade was made easier when Britain entered the Common Market which coincided with the formation of Brittany Ferries in the early 1970s. They were given every assistance by the new ferry company – established by the farmers themselves under the leadership of Alexis Gourvennec. I remember how many of the retired Johnnies would go to the Brittany Ferries offices in Roscoff to telephone Johnnies who were over in Britain selling – telling them that a load of onions was on the way, or to find out how many tons needed to be sent over. They never paid for those telephone calls. But the British pound was getting weaker against the French franc. When it fell below ten francs that was considered to be a disaster – eventually it fell to below seven francs.

The Johnnies who were still coming over were growing older by the mid-60s. There were no new Johnnies between 1939 and 1950. By now, children had to stay longer in school. Anyhow, the social services would never allow a ten-year-old child to spend a winter in damp and draughty warehouse. I remember the late Jean-Marie Roignant telling me – "Sixteen is too late to start being an onion Johnny." They had to learn a new language, and as we know, the younger the better to start learning a new language.

There were other important factors. The Johnnies were not allowed to contribute towards their pensions while they were away in Britain. I knew many a Johnny living on a reduced old age pension because he had spent half a lifetime selling onions in Cardiff or Glasgow. It was the ordinary farm labourers who suffered most – those who worked on the farms around Roscoff and Saint-Pol during the summer before going to sell onions in the autumn. Those who owned a small farm would get round the problem. "I could pay – after all, the authorities never knew where I was," Guillaume Le Duff told me. "For all they knew, I was at home on the farm going about my work."

Opportunities for work improved after the war. If they had to leave home to find work they could find it in the sugar refineries in the Loire valley and around Nantes. At least these factories were within the borders of France – within the limits of Brittany, even. Insurance terms for the Johnnies were not so favourable as for those who stayed at home to work in Brittany and France.

And, of course, the work was hard and the hours were long. There was little comfort living in old condemned shops and crumbling warehouses in a climate that was colder and wetter than that of Roscoff – particularly for those who went to Scotland and the north of England. And the Johnnies were themselves getting older. It seemed unlikely that Johnny Onions would survive to see another century and a new millennium.

Chapter 8

We will remember ...

In spite of the grim prospects at the end of the 1970s and early 1980s, Johnny Onions is still with us. Patrick Mevel and his young company arrive in Cardiff in the middle of August every year. Some of the sellers are students taking a year out to improve their English and Patrick's first task is to teach them the art of stringing and how to *chiner*. Some of them will not return for a second year. And no doubt the old shop they rent in Cardiff's Grangetown is more comfortable than the one Jean-Marie Cueff and Olivier Bertevas had in Bute Street almost 25 years ago. But they still use the bikes, even if they are just props. I have seen one or two bikes without a chain or even tyres! Old traditions have their uses – bicycles, berets, even the striped jerseys.

Even when we look at today's figures - those that I have been able find - the Johnnies still sell a fair percentage of the onions grown in the Roscoff area. Sadly, the red onion of Roscoff is respected more in Britain than in Paris. And without the Johnnies to sell this unique onion, it is in some danger of dying out with the men that sell it. The fewer the Johnnies, the less onions that will be sold. And as the production of onions decreases so does the incentive for the Johnnies.

But even if we rarely see a Breton onion seller in our streets today, the memory lives on. The day the two teams digging the Channel Tunnel met somewhere under the sea between Calais and Dover I saw two newspaper cartoons in which the still familiar image of the Johnnies was used. In one, a row of Johnnies emerged from the tunnel pushing bicycles, handlebars swamped under huge loads of strings of onions. Two workmen look at the onion men and one tells the other, "Looks like we're through, then!"

In another cartoon a man on a bike was speeding through a tunnel, onions on the handlebars, a baguette in one pocket and a bottle of wine sticking out of another passing a notice with the words, "Channel Tunnel, expected breakthrough one mile ahead."

In February 2001 I watched the BBC situation comedy drama series, "Allo, Allo" set in a Paris café run by people who are in the Resistance and frequented by the Germans. In one episode the Germans disguise themselves as French peasants – in other words, Breton onion sellers! The series, I should stress, is made by the BBC for a British audience. And the image of a Frenchman as a Breton onion seller is still recognisable to the average British person, although it would be nonsensical to any French person – even some Bretons find it difficult to understand. In 1999 I recall seeing a well-known Welsh television presenter with a bike and onions in the centre of Paris with the Eiffel Tower in the background. This was neither factually correct nor was it relevant to Paris or any television programme about France. Yet the image of the Breton onion sellers – for well over a hundred years the only "Frenchman" the ordinary Briton was ever likely to meet in his lifetime – still strikes a chord. Many times I have been asked by French people from the south about this image problem. "We can understand the baguettes, the wine – even snails and frogs – but why do you portray us with bicycles and onions?"

I try to explain. "For nearly two centuries men from a small town called Roscoff which is about as far west as you can go in Brittany used to come over to Britain to sell onions. And they carried their onions on bicycles ..." The response I get is either polite, suppressed laughter or their eyes go blank.

My mother told me, after I had seen the first Johnny Onions come to our door in the early 1950s that he could speak Welsh to us because Welsh and Breton were identical languages. Many other Welsh speaking people thought so too. For over a century and a half they kept Wales and Brittany in touch with each other in a time when only the most privileged could afford to make the journey to the other country. François-Alexis Rio and Villemarque created new cultural links with the Reverend Thomas Price (Carnhuanawc) and Lady Llanover at the Abergavenny Eisteddfod in 1838. But the Johnnies, ten years earlier, had planted the seeds of interaction between the working classes – indeed a classless interaction – between the people of Wales and Brittany.

Today more than 30 towns in Wales are twinned with towns in Brittany. It is appropriate to remember that the first Welsh/Breton twinning was that between Saint-Pol-de-Leon and Penarth, near Cardiff. The two towns celebrated a 30-year twinning relationship in 1999 and 2000. The twinning was inspired by Eugène Grall, the boss of a company of Johnnies with their base in Cardiff's docklands. In fact he married in the French consulate in Cardiff. For many years he was the president of the Saint-Pol twinning committee. Since then there have been many more twinnings between Wales and Brittany.

A few years ago I had the honour of working with Madame Patricia Chapalain, the daughter of Eugène Grall, in setting up *La Maison des Johnnies*, the little museum that charts the history of the Johnnies. Madame Chapalain is the owner of the Hotel Brittany and was at the time the deputy mayor of Roscoff. She, too, is proud of her connections with the Johnnies and with Wales.

Establishing the little museum in Roscoff sparked off further interest in the Johnnies. The onion growers section of the SICA *(Société d'Initiative de Coopération Agricole)* began a campaign to persuade supermarkets in Britain to sell bunches of Roscoff onions strung in the way of the Johnnies. Their market has always been in Britain.

So, there is still hope that neither the Johnny nor his onions will be buried just yet. Who knows, that they may still celebrate 200 years since Henri Olivier made his first historic journey. In recent years the pound has been strong against the franc, and even more so the euro. At the moment the situation is favourable for those who are still coming over with their onions. So who knows?

At the time this book was going to press news came that the Roscoff area, because of its onions, is a designated French Site de goût and the onions given appellation contrôlee status – like the wines!

The old Johnnies had warm sentiments towards the people of Britain. When Winston Churchill died, the onion sellers wrote collectively a letter of sympathy to Lady Churchill. "… We owe him our gratitude for all he has done for France in the last war and we cannot forget that it is thanks to him that we are free people today and that we are able to come over to your country to bring you our products … Johnnies de Roscoff."

I mentioned, too, how the Mayor of Southampton and the people of London contributed to the disaster fund when the Hilda sank. In 1953, when the Thames flooded, the Johnnies contributed to the Lord Mayor of London's fund. Likewise the Johnnies contributed to the Aberfan fund when a coal tip slid down the mountain and buried Pantglas Primary School in Merthyr Vale in South Wales in 1967. Over a hundred children and a number of teachers died in the disaster.

There are very few Johnnies now coming over but the memories are of a cheerful, hardworking individual who was part of the everyday experience of most British people for over a century and a half. A character who brought fun and colour into our lives in what was often a grim and grey period.

Some songs and ballads of the onion men

Good onions, very cheap,
Prenit ognon mat
Digant ar Roskoad.
Good onions, very cheap,
Prenit ognon mat
Digant ar Breizad.

Johnniget an ognon
Zo deut euz abell-bro
Da werza d'ar Zaozon
Gwella vouen ogonon 'zo
Da lakat er zouben
Pe gant eun tam rata
Pe gant eur fritaden
Er podig da gana.

Skuiz-maro vont bemdez
Da redet an hentchou
O sevel en tiez
Da skei war an doriou.
Hor c'hein a zo kignet
Dindan ar zam pounner
Hag hor chupen toullet
Zo mat d'ar pilhaouer.

Echuet hon deg leo
Dindad peb amzer fall
E klevomp en distro
Ar Mestr o fraonval.
Ha pa zaimp d'an daoulin
Ha da sonjal pedi
Pe d'an offern vintin
E kwezimp war hor fri,

Prenit 'vit ma c'hellem
Kas d'ar vugaligou
D'ar ger pa zistroimp
Kountellou, muzikou,

Prenit 'vit ma lako
Mylady Marijan
Thé Saoz ken a foeltro
Da virvi war an tan.

Translation

Good onions, very cheap,
Buy good onions.
From the Roscovite;
Good onions, very cheap,
Buy good onions
From the Breton.

Johnny Onions
Came from a distant land
To sell to the English
Onions which are the finest
For putting in the soup
Or on the grill if you wish
Or in the frying pan
Or in the pot to sing.

Dead tired they'll be daily
Trudging the roads
Stopping by the houses
To knock the doors.
Their backs are raw
Beneath their heavy loads
Their coats are torn
And fit for the rag-man.

Finishing our ten miles
In all sorts of filthy weather
And hearing when we return
The boss complaining.
And when we go on our knees
And turn to our prayers
or go to the morning Mass
We could sleep on our noses.

Buy so that I may
Take home to my children
When I return
Toys for counting, toys for music
Buy so that
Milady Marian
Can rush the tea from England
And boil it on the fire.

* * *

Paotred Rosko

N'eus par, e Breiz Izel da baotred Rosko,
Brudet 'int 'vit o nerz dre-holl 'barz ar vro,
Diwallit da goueza dindan o fao,
Ro-sko, sko mibin, sko kallet, sko atao!
Ouspenn, labourerien dispar int ivez,
Da c'houlou-deiz 'maint er maez eus o gwele.
Gwelit o bemdez en aochou tro war dro,
Kerkent ma vo tre, betek ma vo lano,
O pelhiat bezin war ar reier garo,
Rosko, sko mibin, sko kalet, sko atao!

Kalz ijin o deus ivez paotred Rosko,
Eus Bro-C'hall a bez o deus graet an dro,
'Vit gwerza o zrevad dre ar marc'hajo,
Rosko, sko mibin, sko katel, sko atao!
Dre Baris, dre Vro-Zaoz o deus tremenet,
Mont a raint hebdale betek penn ar bed.
Ar Roskoad, gant e vouez skiltr a youc'ho;
'Patatez, brikoli, ougnon, articho!'
'Didabit, kemerit, an neb a garo'
Rosko, sko mibin, sko kalet, sko atao.

N'eus ket lorc'husoc'h eget paotred Rosko,
Gwalenn war' o biz, c'houez vat war o bleo.
Voulouzenn ledan en dro d'ho zog kolo,
Rosko, sko mibin, sko kalet, sko atao.
Gant o dousig pa'z eont d'ar pardoniou,
'Kargont he godell a bep seurt madigou

135

Anaout a reont mad kement dans a zo
Ar ganaouenn ivez 'blij eston d'ezo
Evelse ar merc'hed 'zo pitilh ganto
Rosko, sko mibin, sko kalet, sko atao!

Translation

The Lads of Roscoff

There are no equals in lower Brittany, to the lads of Roscoff,
Celebrated for their strength throughout the land,
Take care you do not fall into their hands
*Rosko, sko mibin, sko kalet, sko atao!
Untiring workers are they who
At the crack of dawn are out of their beds,
Daily you'll see them around the shores
As soon as the tide is out, until it returns
They comb the seaweed from the rocks
*Rosko, sko mibin, sko kalet, sko atao!

Many a guile have the lads of Roscoff,
Through the whole of France have they wandered,
In the markets they peddled their produce,
*Rosko, sko mibin, sko kalet, sko atao!
Through Paris, through England have they tramped,
They'll go to the corners of the world without hesitation
Shouting hoarsely, the lads of Roscoff;
'Potatoes, broccoli, onions, artichokes,
Choose, take, anyone who wishes'.
*Rosko, sko mibin, sko kalet, sko atao.

There are none prouder than the lads of Roscoff,
Rings on their fingers, hair slicked in its place
A wide band of velvet around their straw hats,
*Rosko, sko mibin, sko kalet, sko atao.
With a sweetheart each goes to the Pardons
Filling her pockets with sweet things;

Well do they know every dance
And the songs, too, which will please her,
No wonder the girls all love them.
*Rosko, sko mibin, sko kalet, sko atao.

* This line cannot be adequately translated since it relies on a pun on the
name Rosko (which is the Breton form of Roscoff). Here the name is taken
to mean 'Strike a blow'. Literally, therefore, the whole line translates,
'Strike a blow, a swift blow, a hard blow, a regular blow'.

* * *

La Vie de Johnny

Le jour d'été qu'ils sont partis
Sur un batiment lesté à Rosko,
L'air heureux, on vit les Johnnies
Rire à travers leurs chansons
Et lancer aux gens un gai *kenavo*.
Pour cinq ou six mois très loin ils vont,
Sans trop de bile les attendrons
Et voilà la vie du pauvre cher Johnny.

Au pays saxon à peine arrivés
Et du bâtiment finie la décharge,
Ils s'en vont, un bâton grevé
D'oignons meurtrissont l'épaule,
Sans arrêt, sur les chemins en marge,
Trottant, fourbus, la chair morte,
Tombant parfois, faisant la chine aux portes . . .
Et voilà la vie du pauvre cher Johnny.

Et quand le paquet, par malheur,
Passé midi n'est pas vendu,
De leurs yeux coulent des pleurs,
Car les épaules sont moulues,
Que les oignons ne sont-ils des oranges!
On n'aurait pas tout un jour debattu,
Sans manger, cette marchandise étrange!
Et voilà la vie du pauvre cher Johnny!

Qu'importe le temps, allez, en route!
Que le vent rage ou bien qu'il pleuve!
On dormira tard quoi qu'il en coûte,
Et de bonne heure la couchette sera veuve.
Courage! c'est bientôt la France
Et la retour! En haut les coeurs!
La peine est finie. O douce créance!
Et voilà la vie du pauvre cher Johnny!

Translation

The Life of the Johnny

On the summer's day when they departed
On a ship loaded in Roscoff
Joyful of spirit were the Johnnies
Bellowing and laughing their songs,
Throwing to their friends a gay *'kenavo'*.
They go for five or six long months
With little comfort to await them,
And that's the life of the poor dear Johnny.

In the land of the English, no sooner do they arrive
And the ship has been unloaded
Than they're away, the loaded stick
Of onions bruising their shoulders,
Non-stop, along the road-sides,
Trotting, tripping, senseless with weariness,
Sometimes falling, peddling from door to door . . .
That's the life of the poor dear Johnny.

And when there are strings, alas,
Still unsold after mid-day
The tears run from their eyes
Because their shoulders are bruised.
O that the onions were not oranges!
One would not have to slave all day
Without food, selling this strange merchandise!
That's the life of the poor dear Johnny.

Don't heed the weather, go on your journey,
Let the wind rage or the rain pour!
Late to bed, whatever the price
And early in the morning widowed is the bed.
Courage! before long, France,
And home! And a happy heart!
The pain is over, Sweet the reward!
And that's the life of the poor dear Johnny.

* * *

The Johnnies

(This song was recorded on Ile de Batz)

Dans notre métier, ce n'est pas tout rose
Si l'on a les poches pleines de *pognon*
Pour les récolter c'est une autre chose
Faut voir à l'oeuvre le marchand d'oignons
Courant de portes en portes
Chargés comme des *bourricots*
En attendant que quelqu'un sorte
Pour alléger notre fardeau
Mais c'est encore . . .
Siouaz eun all! chomet a biou.

Et tout le long des rues
s'en va le pauvre Johnnie,
l'air gai, mais l'âme ennuie,
qu'il pleuve, qu'il neige, jour et nuit.
Oui, c'est lui qui *chine*
jusgu'au dernier penny.
C'est le métier de nos Johnnies, à la *chine*
Si par bonheur la chance le favorise.
Il est heureuse comme un poisson dans l'eau
à peine clos, c'est le *bistrot* qu'il vise
pour deguster une bière aussitot.
Redoublant alors de courage,
Il reprend encore son *boulot*
le voila plus gai qui voyage
portant comme un rien son fardeau

confiant la chique à tous ses concurrents
. . . , *eman echu gantan.*

Quand le dimanche où l'on se repose
Tant que l'on veut dans un lit bien chaud
Elle est bien gagneé, cette courte pause
apres 6 jours de *trimand* au galop
Et aussitôt qu'on nous prepare la soupe
Quelque chose d'appetissant,
on joue à 'coeur, figue et je coupe'
Tremen ar zul, eman echu gantan.

Translation

In our trade, life isn't all honey / Even if our pockets are full
of money / It's another matter to get them so / One must see
the onion seller at work / Running from door to door /
Laden like an ass / Waiting for someone to come out / To
lighten his load / But once again . . . / Alas, another! Has
been lost.

Along the streets / Goes the poor Johnny / his appearance is
light but his spirit is low / Be it rain, or snow, day or night.
/ Yes, this one haggling / To the last penny. / That's the
trade of our Johnny, selling from door to door. / If by good
luck fate smiles on him / He is as happy as a fish in water, /
Hardly finished, and its for the pub he goes immediately to
drink a beer. / Then having refreshed his strength / he starts
his work again / There he is happier on his journey /
carrying his load as if it were nothing / getting ahead of his
competition / . . . and then he is gone.

Then on Sunday when one rests / and stays as long as one
wishes in a warm bed / He deserves it, this short break /
after six days of slogging. / And then the soup is prepared
for us / something to raise the appetite, / play our card
game. / Thus the Sunday is spent, and then he is gone.

Appendices

Even when the trade of the Johnnies was at its peak they only imported a small percentage of the onions brought into Britain. The most ever sold at any one period by the Johnnies was 10,000 tons in one year.

These are the average tonnages imported annually into Britain from other countries in the 1960s.

Spain	-	70,000 tons
Holland	-	50,000 tons
Egypt	-	30,000 tons
Canada	-	18,000 tons
Chile	-	15,000 tons
Poland	-	15,000 tons
USA	-	6,000 tons
Hungary	-	5,000 tons

During the same period the annual average or the number of tons imported into Britain by the Johnnies were 3,500.

Number of Johnnies

1860	-	200
1887	-	700
1902	-	1273
1905	-	1152
1907	-	1200
1909	-	1300
1913	-	1000
1921	-	1000
1930	-	1500
1932 – 39	-	700 – 900
1948	-	250
1949	-	75
1955	-	252
1970	-	140
1985	-	33
2000	-	10

Tons of onions exported by the Johnnies to Britain

1860	-	1,000 tons
1908	-	7,906 tons
1913	-	10,000 tons
1921	-	2,572 tons
1927	-	9,710 tons
1931	-	9,710 tons
1932	-	3,245 tons
1933	-	2,786 tons
1936	-	4,500 tons
1937	-	2,203 tons
1947	-	2,500 tons
1963	-	4,500 tons
1966	-	3,000 tons

From 1966 onwards the number of tons exported to Britain continued to decline.

Bibliography

Bebb, W. Ambrose (1941): *Pererindodau*, Y Clwb Llyfau Cymraeg

Griffiths, Gwyn (1987): *Goodbye Johnny Onions*, Dyllansow Truran, Redruth

Griffiths, Gwyn (1996): *Le Johnny, Breton en Grande Bretagne*, Revue Française de Civilisation Britannique, Vol VIII, No 4, Paris

Griffiths, Gwyn (1981): *Y Shonis Olaf*, Gwasg Gomer, Llandysul

Guivarch, François (1979): *Les Johnnies de Roscoff*, Nature de Bretagne, Quimper

Habasque, Celine (1998): *The Johnnies From Their Origin To The Present Day*, Research dissertaton - Université de Bretagne Occidentale, Brest.

Medar, Tad (1986): *Paotred an ognon*, Les Presses Bretonnes, Sant Brieuc

Menez, Jean-Pierre (1986): *Johnnies du Pays de Roscoff hier et aujourd'hui*, Skol Vreizh, Morlaix

Moncus, Jean-Jacques (1973): *L' Émigration saisonnière des Johnnies de Roscoff des origines à nos jours*. Research dissertation - Université de Bretagne Occidentale, Brest

Rozmor, Naig (1998): *Ar Johniged*, Emgleo Breiz, Brest. A play

Rudel, Yves Marie (1945): *Johnny de Roscoff*, Librairie Celtique, Paris. Novel

Saliou, Maryse (1992): *The Johnny Onion Men*. Research dissertation - Université Catholique de l'Ouest, Angers

Acknowledgements

It is thanks to many individuals and organisations that this book has seen the light of day. My thanks go to the late John Owen Huws of the Museum of Welsh Life, Cardiff, for urging me to write it.

Brian Davies, Curator of Pontypridd Museum. His swift agreement that an exhibition of the life of the Johnnies would be of interest made me continue researches which began in the late 70s.

To Michel Morvan, former mayor of Roscoff, who insisted that the town needed a permanent museum in memory of the Johnnies and told me to get on with it.

Patricia Chapalain of the Brittany Hotel, former deputy mayor of Roscoff and the daughter of a Johnny, for her constant support and interest when *La Maison des Johnnies* and the exhibition were being established.

Madeleine Le Guerch for her support, knowledge and the benefit of her brilliant organisational skills.

The Johnnies themselves. To all those mentioned in the book for their friendship, patience and readiness to share memories and experiences. In particular I would mention the Prigent family of Santec.

M. and Mme Robert Simon of Plabennec for their help when I began my researches.

Julian Brown for bringing to my attention the paintings by his great-grandfather, Ralph Hedley, which have provided such a splendid cover for the book.

Brittany Ferries for their practical support over the years.

To the present mayor of Roscoff, Monsieur Seité, and the staff of the Hôtel de Ville for their continuing interest and support.

Finally, my thanks to Myrddin ap Dafydd of Gwasg Carreg Gwalch and Michel Tanguy and Josseline Mondot of Les Editions Le Télégramme for their enthusiasm, advice and an attractive book.

Gwyn Griffiths